Introduction to Buddhism

Also by Geshe Kelsang Gyatso

Meaningful to Behold
Clear Light of Bliss
Heart of Wisdom
Universal Compassion
Joyful Path of Good Fortune
Guide to Dakini Land
The Bodhisattva Vow
Heart Jewel
Great Treasury of Merit
Understanding the Mind
Tantric Grounds and Paths
Ocean of Nectar
Essence of Vajrayana
Living Meaningfully, Dying Joyfully
Eight Steps to Happiness
Transform Your Life
The New Meditation Handbook
How to Solve Our Human Problems
Mahamudra Tantra

Profits received by Tharpa Publications from
the sale of this book will be donated to the
NKT-IKBU International Temples Project
Part of the New Kadampa Tradition
A Nonprofit Buddhist Organization,
Building for World Peace
www.kadampa.org/temples.htm

GESHE KELSANG GYATSO

Introduction to Buddhism

AN EXPLANATION OF THE BUDDHIST WAY OF LIFE

THARPA PUBLICATIONS
USA UK CANADA
AUSTRALIA HONG KONG

Published 2008
First UK edition published 1992

Tharpa Publications
47 Sweeney Road
Glen Spey, NY 12737
USA

Tharpa Publications
Conishead Priory
Ulverston
Cumbria LA12 9QQ, England

Tharpa Publications has offices around the world,
and our books are available in most major languages.
See page 191 for more information.

© New Kadampa Tradition—International Kadampa Buddhist Union 2008

Cover illustration by Robert Beer.
Line illustrations by Sarah Young.

Library of Congress Control Number: 2007906848

ISBN-13 978-0-9789067-6-4 hardback
ISBN-10 0-9789067-6-4 hardback

ISBN-13 978-0-9789067-7-1 paperback
ISBN-10 0-9789067-7-2 paperback

ISBN-13 978-0-9789067-8-8 audio book
ISBN-10 0-9789067-8-0 audio book

Set in Adobe Garamond Pro by Tharpa Publications USA.
Printed in the United States of America on acid-free paper.

Contents

Illustrations

The illustrations in this book depict the Thirty-five Confession Buddhas. The purification practice associated with these Confession Buddhas, called *Mahayana Sutra of the Three Superior Heaps*, is explained in Appendix II.

Acknowledgements

*T*his book, *Introduction to Buddhism*, is an exceptionally clear explanation of the Buddhist way of life. From the depths of our hearts we thank the author, Venerable Geshe Kelsang Gyatso, for his immeasurable kindness in preparing this book, which provides a definitive introduction to Buddhism for those in the West.

We also thank all the dedicated, senior Dharma students who assisted the author with the rendering of the English and who prepared the final manuscript for publication.

Roy Tyson,
Administrative Director,
Manjushri Kadampa
Meditation Center

Editorial Note

If you are not already familiar with the life and teachings of Buddha, you may find some of the concepts and practices introduced in this book a little unusual to begin with. However, if you think about them patiently and sincerely, you will discover that they are very meaningful and have great relevance to our daily lives. Although Buddhism is an ancient religion that first appeared in the East, the practices taught by Buddha are timeless and universally applicable. These days, many people are discovering that Buddhism has answers to questions and solutions to problems that cannot be found anywhere else. It is hoped, therefore, that the publication of this book will help to deepen the understanding and appreciation of Buddhism in the West.

Cover illustration The lotus flower is a traditional Buddhist symbol of purity. A lotus is born from the mud at the bottom of a lake but blossoms above the water as a stainless flower that brings pleasure to all who see it. In a similar fashion, living beings are born in the ocean of suffering with impure bodies and impure minds, but if they train in meditation they can attain a completely pure body and mind, and bring peace and happiness to all who meet them.

PART ONE

Basic Buddhism

Buddha Shakyamuni

Who Was Buddha?

In general, *Buddha* means "Awakened One," someone who has awakened from the sleep of ignorance and sees things as they really are. A Buddha is a person who is completely free from all faults and mental obstructions. There are many people who have become Buddhas in the past, and many people will become Buddhas in the future.

The Buddha who is the founder of the Buddhist religion is called Buddha Shakyamuni. *Shakya* is the name of the royal family he was born into, and *Muni* means "Able One." Buddha Shakyamuni was born as a royal prince in 624 BC in a place called Lumbini, which was originally in northern India but is now part of Nepal. His mother's name was Queen Mayadevi and his father's name was King Shuddhodana.

One night, Queen Mayadevi dreamed that a white elephant descended from heaven and entered her womb. The white elephant entering her womb indicated that on that very night she had conceived a child who was a pure and powerful being. The elephant's descending from heaven indicated that her child came from Tushita heaven, the Pure Land of Buddha Maitreya. Later, when she gave birth to the child, instead of experiencing pain the queen experienced a special, pure vision in which she stood holding the branch of a tree with her right hand while the gods Brahma and Indra took the child painlessly from her side. They then proceeded to honor the infant by offering him ritual ablutions.

When the king saw the child, he felt as if all his wishes had been fulfilled and he named the young prince "Siddhartha." He invited a Brahmin seer to make predictions about the prince's future. The seer examined the child with his clairvoyance and told the king, "There are signs that the boy could become either a chakravatin king, a ruler of the entire world, or a fully enlightened Buddha. However, since the time for chakravatin kings is now past, it is certain that he will become a Buddha, and that his beneficial influence will pervade the thousand million worlds like the rays of a sun."

As the young prince grew up, he mastered all the traditional arts and sciences without needing any instruction. He knew sixty-four different languages, each with its own alphabet, and he was also very skilled at mathematics. He once told his father that he could count all the atoms in the world in the time it takes to draw a single breath. Although he did not need to study, he did so to please his father and to benefit others. At his father's request, he joined a school where, in addition to studying various academic subjects, he became skilled at sports such as martial arts and archery.

The prince would take every opportunity to convey spiritual meanings and to encourage others to follow spiritual paths. At one time, when he was taking part in an archery contest, he declared, "With the bow of meditative concentration, I will fire the arrow of wisdom and kill the tiger of ignorance in living beings." He then re-

Seeing how all living beings are trapped in this vicious circle of suffering, he developed a sincere wish to free them.

leased the arrow and it flew straight through five iron tigers and seven trees before disappearing into the earth! By witnessing demonstrations such as this, thousands of people developed faith in the prince.

Sometimes Prince Siddhartha would go into the capital city of his father's kingdom to see how the people lived. During these visits, he came into contact with many old people and sick people, and on one occasion he saw a corpse. These encounters left a deep impression on his mind and led him to realize that all living beings without exception have to experience the sufferings of birth, sickness, aging, and death. Because he understood the laws of reincarnation, he also realized that living beings experience these sufferings not just once, but again and again, in life after life without cessation. Seeing how all living beings are trapped in this vicious circle of suffering, he felt deep compassion for them, and he developed a sincere wish to free all of them from their suffering. Realizing that only a fully enlightened Buddha has the wisdom and the power to help all living beings in this way, he resolved to leave the palace and retire to the solitude of the forest where he would engage in profound meditation until he attained enlightenment.

When the people of the Shakya kingdom realized that the prince intended to leave the palace, they requested the king to arrange a marriage for him in the hope that this would cause him to change his mind. The king agreed and soon found him a suitable bride, the daughter of a respected Shakya family, named Yasodhara. Prince Siddhartha, however, had no attachment to worldly pleasures because he realized that objects of attachment are like poisonous flowers, which initially appear to be attractive but eventually give rise to great pain. His resolve to leave the palace and to attain enlightenment remained unchanged, but to fulfill his father's wishes, and to bring temporary benefit to the Shakya people, he agreed to marry Yasodhara. However, even though he remained in the palace as a royal prince, he devoted all his time and energy to serving the Shakya people in whatever way he could.

When he was twenty-nine years old, the prince had a vision in which all the Buddhas of the ten directions appeared to him and spoke in unison, saying, "Previously you resolved to become a Conqueror Buddha so that you could help all living beings trapped in the cycle of suffering. Now is the time for you to accomplish this." The prince went immediately to his parents and told them of his intention, "I wish to retire to a peaceful place in the forest where I can engage in deep meditation and quickly attain full enlightenment. Once I have attained enlightenment, I will be able to repay the kindness of all living beings, and especially the great kindness that you have shown me. Therefore, I request your permission to leave the palace." When his parents heard this, they were shocked, and the king refused to grant his permission. Prince Siddhartha said to his father, "Father, if you can give me permanent freedom from the sufferings of birth, sickness, aging, and death, I will stay in the palace. But if you cannot, I must leave and make my human life meaningful."

The king tried all means to prevent his son from leaving the palace. In the hope that the prince might change his mind, he surrounded him with a retinue of beautiful women, dancers, singers, and musicians, who day and night used their charms to please him. In case the prince might attempt a secret escape, he posted guards around the palace walls. However, the prince's determination to leave the palace and enter a life of meditation could not be shaken. One night he used his miracle powers to send the guards and attendants into a deep sleep while he made his escape from the palace with the help of a trusted aide. After they had traveled about six miles, the prince dismounted from his horse and said goodbye to his aide. He then cut off his hair and threw it into the sky, where it was caught by the gods of the Land of the Thirty-three Heavens. One of the gods then offered the prince the saffron robes of a religious mendicant. The prince accepted these and gave his royal garments to the god in exchange. In this way, he ordained himself as a monk.

Siddhartha then made his way to a place near Bodh Gaya in India, where he found a suitable site for meditation. There he remained, emphasizing a meditation called *space-like concentration on the Dharmakaya*, in which he focused single-pointedly on the ultimate nature of all phenomena. After training in this meditation for six years, he realized that he was very close to attaining full enlightenment, and so he walked to Bodh Gaya where, on the full moon day of the fourth month of the lunar calendar, he seated himself beneath the Bodhi Tree in the meditation posture and vowed not to rise from meditation until he had attained perfect enlightenment. With this determination, he entered the space-like concentration on the Dharmakaya.

As dusk fell, Devaputra Mara, the chief of all the demons, or maras, in this world, tried to disturb Siddhartha's concentration by conjuring up many frightening apparitions. He manifested hosts of terrifying demons—some throwing spears, some firing arrows, some trying to burn him with fire, and some hurling boulders and even mountains at him. Siddhartha, however, remained completely undisturbed. Through the force of his concentration, the weapons, rocks, and mountains appeared to him as a rain of fragrant flowers, and the raging fires became like offerings of rainbow light.

Seeing that Siddhartha could not be frightened into abandoning his meditation, Devaputra Mara instead tried to distract him by manifesting countless beautiful women, but Siddhartha responded by developing even deeper concentration. In this way he triumphed over all the demons of this world, which is why he subsequently became known as a *Conqueror Buddha*.

Siddhartha then continued with his meditation until dawn, when he attained the vajra-like concentration. With this concentration, which is the very last mind of a limited being, he removed the final veils of ignorance from his mind and in the next moment became a Buddha, a fully enlightened being.

There is nothing that Buddha does not know. Because he has awakened from the sleep of ignorance and has removed all obstructions from his mind, he knows everything of the past, present, and future, directly and simultaneously. In addition, Buddha has great compassion that is completely impartial, embracing all living beings without discrimination. He benefits all living beings without exception by emanating various forms throughout the universe and by bestowing his blessings on their minds. Through receiving Buddha's blessings, all beings, even the lowliest animals, sometimes develop peaceful and virtuous states of mind. Eventually, through meeting an emanation of Buddha in the form of a Spiritual Guide, everyone will have the opportunity to enter the path to liberation and enlightenment. As the great Indian Buddhist scholar Nagarjuna said, there is no one who has not received help from Buddha.

Forty-nine days after Buddha attained enlightenment, the gods Brahma and Indra requested him to teach, saying:

O Buddha, Treasure of Compassion,
Living beings are like blind people in constant
    danger of falling into the lower realms.
Other than you there is no Protector in this world.
Therefore we beseech you, please rise from medita-
    tive equipoise and turn the Wheel of Dharma.

As a result of this request, Buddha rose from meditation and taught the first Wheel of Dharma. These teachings, which include the *Sutra of the Four Noble Truths* and other discourses, are the principal source of the Hinayana, or Lesser Vehicle, of Buddhism. Later, Buddha taught the second and third Wheels of Dharma, which include the *Perfection of Wisdom Sutras* and the *Sutra Discriminating the Intention*, respectively. These teachings are the source of the Mahayana, or Great Vehicle, of Buddhism. In the Hinayana teachings, Buddha explains how to attain liberation from suffering for oneself alone. In the Mahayana teachings, he explains how to attain full enlightenment, or Buddhahood, for the sake of others. Both traditions flourished in Asia, at first in India and then gradually in other surrounding countries, including Tibet. Now they are also beginning to flourish in the West.

The reason why Buddha's teachings are called the *Wheel of Dharma* is as follows. It is said that in ancient times there

MATH 107 MATH MATH

were great kings, known as *chakravatin kings*, who used to rule the entire world. These kings had many special posses-

sions, including a precious wheel in which they would travel around the world. Wherever the precious wheel went, the king would control that

Without inner peace, outer peace is impossible.

region. Buddha's teachings are said to be like a precious wheel, because wherever they spread, the people in that area have the opportunity to control their minds by putting them into practice.

Dharma means "protection." By practicing Buddha's teachings, we protect ourself from suffering and problems. All the problems we experience during daily life originate in ignorance, and the method for eliminating ignorance is to practice Dharma.

Practicing Dharma is the supreme method for improving the quality of our human life. The quality of life depends not on external development or material progress, but on the inner development of peace and happiness. For example, in the past many Buddhists lived in poor and underdeveloped countries, but they were able to find pure, lasting happiness by practicing what Buddha had taught.

If we integrate Buddha's teachings into our daily life, we will be able to solve all our inner problems and attain a truly peaceful mind. Without inner peace, outer peace is impossible. If we first establish peace within our minds by training in spiritual paths, outer peace will come naturally;

but if we do not, world peace will never be achieved, no matter how many people campaign for it.

Buddhism, or Buddhadharma, is Buddha's teachings and the inner experiences or realizations of these teachings. Buddha gave eighty-four thousand teachings. All these teachings and the inner realizations of them constitute Buddhism. Buddhism can be divided into two parts: basic Buddhism and advanced Buddhism. The essential teachings of basic Buddhism are now explained in the remainder of Part One of this book, and the more advanced teachings are introduced in Parts Two and Three.

Understanding the $\mathcal{M}$*ind*

$\mathcal{B}$uddha taught that everything depends on the mind. To realize this, we must first understand the nature and functions of the mind. At first, this might seem straightforward since we all have minds and we all know what state our mind is in—whether it is happy or sad, clear or confused, and so on. However, if someone asked us what the nature of our mind is and how it functions, we would probably not be able to give a precise answer. This indicates that we do not have a clear understanding of the mind.

Some people think that the mind is the brain or some other part or function of the body, but this is incorrect. The brain is a physical object that can be seen with the eyes and that can be photographed or operated on in surgery. The mind, on the other hand, is not a physical object. It cannot be seen with the eyes, photographed or repaired by surgery. The brain, therefore, is not the mind but simply part of the body.

There is nothing within the body that can be identified as being our mind because our body and mind are different

Buddha Complete Subduer
with the Essence of Vajra

Buddha Jewel of
Radiant Light

Buddha Powerful
King of the Nagas

entities. For example, sometimes when our body is relaxed and immobile, our mind can be very busy, darting from one object to another. This indicates that our body and mind are not the same entity. In the Buddhist scriptures, our body is compared to a guesthouse and our mind to a guest residing within it. When we die, our mind leaves our body and goes to the next life, just like a guest leaving a guesthouse and going somewhere else.

If the mind is not the brain, or any other part of the body, what is it? It is a formless continuum that functions to perceive and understand objects. Because the mind is formless, or non-physical, by nature, it is not obstructed by physical objects. For example, it is impossible for our body to go to the moon without traveling in a spaceship, but our mind can reach the moon in an instant just by thinking about it. Knowing and perceiving objects is the uncommon function of the mind. Although we say, "I know such and such," in reality it is our mind that knows. We know things only by using our mind.

There are three levels of mind: gross, subtle, and very subtle. Gross minds include sense awarenesses such as eye awareness and ear awareness, and all strong delusions such as anger, jealousy, attachment, and strong self-grasping ignorance. These gross minds are related to gross inner winds and are relatively easy to recognize. When we fall asleep or die, our gross minds dissolve inward and our subtle minds become manifest. Subtle minds are related to subtle inner winds and are more difficult to recognize than gross minds. During deep sleep, and at the end of the death process, the inner winds dissolve into the center of the heart channel wheel inside the central channel, and then the very subtle mind, the mind of clear light, becomes manifest. The very subtle mind is related to the very subtle inner wind and is extremely difficult to recognize. The continuum of the very subtle mind has no beginning and no end. It is this mind that goes from one life to the next, and if it is completely purified by training in meditation, it is this mind that will eventually transform into the omniscient mind of a Buddha.

It is very important to be able to distinguish between unpeaceful states of mind and peaceful states. States of mind that disturb our inner peace, such as anger, jealousy, and desirous attachment, are called *delusions*. These are the principal causes of all our suffering. We may think that our suffering is caused by other people, by poor material conditions, or by society, but in reality it all comes from our own deluded states of mind. The essence of Dharma practice is to reduce and eventually to completely eradicate our delusions, and to replace them with peaceful, virtuous states of mind. This is the main purpose of training in meditation.

Normally we seek happiness outside ourself. We try to obtain better material conditions, a better job, higher social status, and so on; but no matter how successful we are in improving our external situation, we still experience many problems and much dissatisfaction. We never experience pure, lasting happiness. In his Dharma teachings, Buddha advises us not to seek happiness outside ourself but to establish it within our mind. How can we do this? By purifying and controlling our mind through the sincere practice of Buddhadharma. If we train in this way, we can ensure that our mind remains calm and happy all the time. Then, no matter how difficult our external circumstances may be, we will always be happy and peaceful.

Even though we work very hard to find happiness, it remains elusive for us, while sufferings and problems seem to come naturally, without any effort. Why is this? It is because the cause of happiness within our mind—virtue—is very weak and can give rise to its effect only if we apply

Buddha advises us not to seek happiness outside ourself but to establish it within our mind.

great effort, while the internal causes of suffering and problems—delusions—are very strong and can give rise to their effects with no effort on our part. This is the real reason why problems come naturally while happiness is so difficult to find.

From this we can see that the principal causes of both happiness and problems are in the mind, not in the external world. If we were able to maintain a calm and peaceful mind all day long, we would never experience any problems or mental suffering. For example, if our mind remains peaceful all the time, then even if we are insulted, criticized, or blamed, or if we lose our job or our friends, we will not become unhappy. No matter how difficult our external circumstances may become, as long as we maintain a calm and peaceful mind, the situation will not be a problem for us. Therefore, if we wish to be free from problems there is only one thing to do—learn to maintain a peaceful state of mind by practicing Dharma sincerely and purely.

Past and Future Lives

If we understand the nature of the mind, we can also understand the existence of past and future lives. Many people believe that when the body disintegrates at death, the continuum of the mind ceases and the mind becomes non-existent, like a candle flame going out when all the wax has burned. There are even some people who contemplate committing suicide in the hope that if they die their problems and sufferings will end. However, these ideas are completely wrong. As already explained, our body and mind are separate entities, so even though the body disintegrates at death, the continuum of the mind remains unbroken. Instead of ceasing, the mind simply leaves the present body and goes to the next life. For ordinary beings, therefore, instead of releasing us from suffering, death only brings new sufferings. Not understanding this, many people destroy their precious human life by committing suicide.

One way to gain an understanding of past and future lives is to examine the process of sleeping, dreaming, and waking, because this closely resembles the process of death,

Buddha Leader of the Heroes

Buddha Glorious Pleasure

Buddha Jewel Fire

intermediate state, and rebirth. When we fall asleep, our gross inner winds gather and dissolve inward, and our mind becomes progressively more and more subtle until it transforms into the very subtle mind of the clear light of sleep. While the clear light of sleep is manifest, we experience deep sleep, and to others we resemble a dead person. When the clear light of sleep ends, our mind gradually becomes more and more gross and we pass through the various levels of the dream state. Finally, our normal powers of memory and mental control are restored and we wake up. When this happens, our dream world disappears and we perceive the world of the waking state.

A very similar process occurs when we die. As we die, our winds dissolve inward and our mind becomes progressively more and more subtle until the very subtle mind of the clear light of death becomes manifest. The experience of the clear light of death is very similar to the experience of deep sleep. After the clear light of death has ceased, we experience the stages of the intermediate state, or *bardo* in Tibetan, which is a dream-like state that occurs between death and rebirth. After a few days or weeks, the intermediate state ends and we take rebirth. Just as when we awaken from sleep, the dream world disappears and we perceive the world of the waking state, so when we take rebirth, the appearances of the intermediate state cease and we perceive the world of our next life.

The only significant difference between the process of

sleeping, dreaming, and waking and the process of death, intermediate state, and rebirth is that after the clear light of sleep has ceased, the relationship between our mind and our present body remains intact, while after the clear light of death this relationship is broken. By contemplating this, we will gain conviction in the existence of past and future lives.

We generally believe that the things we perceive in dreams are unreal while the things we perceive when we are awake are true; but Buddha said that all phenomena are like dreams in that they are mere appearances to mind. For those who can interpret them correctly, dreams have great significance. For example, if we dream that we visit a particular country that we have never been to in this life, our dream will indicate one of four things: that we have been to that country in a previous life, that we will visit it later in this life, that we will visit it in a future life, or that it has some personal significance for us, as it would, for example, if we had recently received a letter from that country or had seen a television program about it. Similarly, if we dream we are flying, it may mean that in a previous life we were a being who could fly, such as a bird or a meditator with miracle powers, or it may predict that we will become such a being in the future. A flying dream may also have a less literal meaning, symbolizing an improvement in our health or state of mind.

All phenomena are like dreams in that they are mere appearances to mind.

It was with the help of dreams that I was able to discover where my mother had been reborn after she had died. Just before she died, my mother dozed off for a few minutes and when she woke she told my sister, who was caring for her, that she had dreamed of me and that in her dream I had offered her a traditional white scarf, or *khatag*. I believed this dream to mean that I would be able to help my mother in her next life, and so after she died, I prayed every day for her to be reborn in England, where I was living, so that I would have the opportunity to meet and recognize her reincarnation. I made strong requests to my Dharmapala to show me clear signs of where my mother's reincarnation could be found.

Later, I had three dreams that seemed to be significant. In the first, I dreamed that I met my mother in a place I believed was England. I asked her how she had traveled from India to England, but she replied that she had not come from India but from Switzerland. In the second dream, I saw my mother talking to a group of people. I approached her and spoke to her in Tibetan, but she did not seem to understand what I was saying. While she was alive, my mother spoke only Tibetan, but in this dream she spoke English fluently. I asked her why she had forgotten Tibetan, but she did not reply. Later in the same dream, I dreamed of a Western couple who are helping with the development of Dharma Centers in England.

Both dreams seemed to give clues about where my mother had been reborn. Two days after the second dream, the husband of the couple I had dreamed of visited me and told me that his wife was pregnant. I immediately remembered my dream and thought that her baby might be my mother's reincarnation. The fact that in the dream my mother had forgotten Tibetan and spoke only English suggested that she would be reborn in an English-speaking country, and the presence of this couple in the dream might have been an indication that they were her parents. I then performed a traditional divination together with ritual prayers, and this indicated that their child was my mother's reincarnation. I was very happy but did not say anything to anyone.

One night I dreamed about my mother again and again. The next morning, I considered the matter carefully and reached a decision. If the baby had been born that night, then it was definitely my mother's reincarnation, but if it had not, I would need to check further. Having made this decision, I phoned the husband, who gave me the good news that his wife had given birth to a baby girl the previous night. I was delighted and performed a puja, or offering ceremony, as a thanksgiving to my Dharmapala.

A few days later, the father phoned and told me that if he recited the mantra of Buddha Avalokiteshvara, OM MANI PÄME HUM, when the baby cried, she would immediately stop crying and appear to be listening to the mantra. He asked me why this was, and I replied that it was because of her tendencies from her previous life. I knew that my mother had recited this mantra with strong faith throughout her life.

The child was named Amaravajra. Later, when my mother's brother, Kuten Lama, visited England and saw Amaravajra for the first time, he was astonished by how affectionate she was toward him. He said that it was as if she recognized him. I also had the same experience. Although I was able to visit the young child only occasionally, she was always extremely happy to see me.

When Amaravajra started to talk, one day she pointed to a dog and said, "kyi, kyi." After this, she used to say "kyi" many times whenever she saw a dog. Her father asked me if "kyi" meant anything, and I told him that in the dialect of western Tibet, where my mother used to live, "kyi" means "dog." This was not the only Tibetan word the little girl uttered spontaneously.

I later heard through my sister's husband that, after my mother's death, a Tibetan astrologer had predicted that my mother would be born as a female in a country with a language other than Tibetan. This story comes from my own personal experience, but if we investigate we can find many other true stories about how people have been able to recognize the reincarnations of their Teachers, parents, friends, and others. If we contemplate such stories, and reflect on the nature of the mind and the experience of dreams, we will definitely become convinced of the existence of past and future lives.

In his Tantric teachings, Buddha taught a special practice called *transference of consciousness into another body*. This practice became quite widespread in the early days of Buddhism in Tibet. One practitioner who mastered it was Tarma Dode, the son of the famous Tibetan lay Lama and translator, Marpa. One day, while riding a horse, Tarma Dode fell and fatally injured his body. Knowing that his son had mastered the practice of transference of consciousness, Marpa immediately began searching for a corpse into which Tarma Dode could transfer his consciousness. Unable to find a human corpse, Marpa brought his son a pigeon's corpse, which would serve as a temporary home for his mind until he could find a suitable human corpse. Tarma Dode then ejected his mind from his dying human body and entered into the corpse of the pigeon. Immediately, Tarma Dode's old human body died and the pigeon's body came back to life. Tarma Dode's body was now the body of a pigeon, but his mind was still the mind of a human being.

Since he did not want his son to remain in the form of a pigeon, Marpa continued to search for a qualified human corpse. One day, with his clairvoyance, he saw that a Buddhist Teacher had just died in India and that his disciples had taken his corpse to the cemetery. Marpa told his son to fly to India as quickly as possible. Tarma Dode then flew to India in his pigeon's body, and when he arrived at the place where the Teacher's corpse had been left, he ejected his mind from the pigeon's body and entered the corpse.

The body of the pigeon immediately died and the body of the deceased Teacher came back to life. Tarma Dode then spent the remainder of his life as an Indian Teacher known as Tiwu Sangngak Dongpo. Some years later, Marpa's principal disciple, Milarepa, sent his own disciple, Rechungpa, to India to receive special teachings from Tiwu Sangngak Dongpo. When Rechungpa returned to Tibet, he offered these instructions to Milarepa.

There are many other examples of past meditators who could transfer their consciousness into other bodies. It is said that Marpa himself practiced transference of consciousness into another body four times during his life. If mind and body were the same entity, how would it be possible for these meditators to transfer their consciousness in this way? If we contemplate true stories such as these with a positive mind, it will help us understand how it is possible for consciousness to continue beyond the death of the body. This in turn will make it very easy for us to understand the existence of past and future lives.

Buddha Jewel Moonlight

Buddha Meaningful to Behold   *Buddha Jewel Moon*

What Is Karma?

To understand the laws that govern rebirth from one life to another, we need to understand karma. *Karma* is a Sanskrit term meaning "action." All intentional bodily, verbal, and mental actions are karma. Sometimes when Buddhists experience suffering or misfortune, they say, "This is my karma," and accept it patiently. Strictly speaking, however, the suffering we experience is not actual karma but the effect of karma we have accumulated either in previous lives or earlier in this life.

All bodily and verbal actions depend on mental actions because they are all preceded by a mental intention to act. Without an intention to act, we would not do anything. A mental intention that is a determination to perform an action is a mental action or mental karma. Thus, bodily karma is bodily activity initiated by a mental action, and verbal karma is verbal activity initiated by a mental action. From this we can see that mental karma is more important than either bodily karma or verbal karma.

Whether an action is good, bad, or neutral depends principally on the intention that motivates it. Good actions come from good intentions, bad actions from bad intentions, and neutral actions from neutral intentions. Good, or virtuous, actions are the main cause of rebirth in the higher realms, and of future happiness, while bad, or non-virtuous, actions are the main cause of rebirth in the lower realms, and of future suffering. This dependent relationship between actions and effects, virtuous actions causing happiness and non-virtuous actions causing suffering, is taught by the Buddhas based on their perfect knowledge. We must believe it because conviction in the laws of karma is the root of future happiness.

Our mind is like a field, and performing actions is like sowing seeds in that field.

Every action we perform leaves an imprint on our very subtle mind, and each imprint eventually gives rise to its own effect. Our mind is like a field, and performing actions is like sowing seeds in that field. Virtuous actions sow seeds of future happiness and non-virtuous actions sow seeds of future suffering. These seeds remain dormant in our mind until the conditions for them to ripen occur, and then they produce their effect. In some cases, this can happen many lifetimes after the original action was performed.

The seeds that ripen when we die are very important because they determine what kind of rebirth we will take in the next life. Which particular seed ripens at death depends on the state of mind in which we die. If we die with a peaceful mind, this will stimulate a virtuous seed and we will experience a fortunate rebirth. However, if we die with an unpeaceful mind, such as in a state of anger, this will stimulate a non-virtuous seed and we will experience an unfortunate rebirth. This is similar to the way in which nightmares are triggered by our being in an agitated state of mind just before falling asleep.

There are six realms in which it is possible to take rebirth: three lower realms and three higher realms. The three lower realms are the animal realm, the hungry spirit realm, and the hell realm. The three higher realms are the human realm, the demi-god realm, and the god realm. These are described in more detail in *The New Meditation Handbook*.

Virtuous actions, or good karma, are the main cause not only of rebirth in the higher realms of humans and gods, but also of happiness and good fortune in general. Thus, if things go well for us in this life—if we have good health, comfortable living conditions, and good relationships with others, or if we meet with success in our activities—this is our previous good karma ripening. Similarly, success in our spiritual practice, and all our spiritual attainments, are the result of virtuous karma. On the other hand, all the suffering we experience in this life, such as sickness, poverty, conflict, accidents, and harm from human beings and non-human beings, is the result of our own past negative karma. If our deepest wishes remain unfulfilled while the things we dislike appear with ease, or if we fail to find good friends, or having found them, we are soon separated from them, these too are due to the ripening of our past negative karma. Even minor annoyances such as interferences in our daily routine, or the discontent that underlies so much of our life, are the result of the non-virtuous karma accumulated in previous lives.

From this we can see that if we want protection from suffering and from the danger of lower rebirth, we must try not to commit any more negative karma, and we must also try to purify the negative karma that we have already committed. There are ten principal non-virtuous actions that we should avoid: three actions of the body, four of speech, and three of the mind. The three non-virtuous bodily actions are killing, stealing, and sexual misconduct; the four non-virtuous verbal actions are lying, divisive speech, hurtful speech, and idle chatter; and the three non-virtuous mental actions are covetousness, malice, and holding wrong views. These are explained fully in *Joyful Path of Good Fortune*.

The best way to avoid committing negative actions is to practice consideration for others. Since everyone, even animals and insects, wants to be happy and does not want to experience suffering, we should try never to harm any living being. If we kill even a tiny insect, this is a non-virtuous action because it causes great suffering to the insect. We may enjoy fishing, but if we consider this action from the point of view of the fish, we will realize how harmful it is. We need to develop compassion for human beings and animals alike, without discrimination; and we should be extremely careful not to cause suffering to any living being.

All non-virtuous actions have three kinds of effect: the ripened effect, the effect similar to the cause, and the environmental effect. The ripened effect of a negative action is rebirth in one of the three lower realms. The most severe negative actions ripen as rebirth in the hell realm, less severe negative actions as rebirth in the hungry spirit realm, and the least severe negative actions as rebirth in the animal realm.

There are two kinds of effect that are similar to the cause: tendencies similar to the cause and experiences similar to the cause. These two effects are further repercussions of a non-virtuous action that are experienced after the ripened effect has finished and we have taken another rebirth in any of the six realms.

A tendency similar to the cause is a strong compulsion to repeat similar non-virtuous actions. This effect makes it very difficult for us to avoid committing further negative actions, and thereby creating the cause to take even more lower rebirths in the future. The tendency similar to the action of killing is to have a tendency to kill. For example, when some people see a spider in their room they automatically respond by crushing it, and there are some children who cannot resist tormenting or torturing animals. These are tendencies that resemble destructive actions committed in the past. Similarly, the tendency resembling the action of sexual misconduct is to feel strongly attracted to other people's partners.

The effects that are experiences similar to the ten non-virtuous actions are as follows. The experience similar to killing is that our life is short and full of sickness and disease. By killing, we shorten someone else's life and so we ourself experience a short life and poor health. If we are experiencing such things in this life, we can know for certain that they are the results of our own previous negative actions. The experience similar to stealing is that we lack wealth and possessions, and when we do manage to gather some, they are stolen from us or people borrow them and fail to return them. The experience similar to sexual misconduct is that we are quickly separated from our friends and family, our partners abandon us for someone else, the people who work for us soon resign, and we experience loneliness. We can see that some people who are old and ugly have many friends and a devoted partner, while others who are young and beautiful cannot find a loyal partner or lasting friendships.

The experience similar to lying is that no one trusts what we say and people do not listen to our advice. The experience similar to divisive speech is that we find it hard to develop harmonious relationships with others. The experience similar to hurtful speech is that others say unpleasant things to us and speak badly about us. Whenever someone hurts us by speaking offensively or sarcastically, we can recognize this as the result of our own previous harsh words.

The experience similar to idle chatter is that people do not take seriously what we say. They regard us as foolish and do not pay attention to our comments and opinions.

The experience similar to covetousness is that our desires are not fulfilled and we fail to obtain what we want. The experience similar to malice is that we are constantly prone to fear and we panic in dangerous situations. The experience similar to holding wrong views is that we have great confusion and find it difficult to develop wisdom. In addition, when we hear or read Dharma, we are full of doubt. If we now find it hard to remove misconceptions and attain spiritual realizations, this is the result of our clinging to wrong views in the past.

The third effect of a negative action is the environmental effect. Generally, this means that when we take another human rebirth, for example, our environment and the things that surround us are hostile, dangerous, or uncomfortable. The environmental effect of killing is that the place where we live is poor and it is hard to find food and other necessities. The environmental effect of stealing is that the place where we live is barren, and plants and crops will not flourish there. The environmental effect of sexual misconduct is that the place where we live is unclean and breeds disease.

The environmental effect of lying is that we live in a place where people cheat and deceive us, and where there is no one we can trust. The environmental effect of divisive speech is that the place where we live is rugged and mountainous, and there is little transportation so people have to carry heavy loads. Since divisive speech makes smooth and harmonious relationships between people difficult, we have to inhabit a hard and inhospitable environment where communications are difficult to establish. The environmental effect of hurtful speech is that we have to live in a place where there is dense undergrowth, or plants that sting and tear our flesh, causing us discomfort whenever we move around. The environmental effect of idle chatter is that we live in a place where fruit and crops do not grow properly or at the right time, and so they are wasted.

The environmental effect of covetousness is that we have to live in a place where material resources are easily destroyed or lost, or where our bodily strength and beauty quickly degenerate. The environmental effect of malice is that we are reborn in a place that is ravaged by war and disease, or where there is continuous conflict. The environmental effect of holding wrong views is that we are reborn in a place that lacks water and where resources are quickly exhausted. It is a place where nothing precious exists—no works of art, no valuable treasures, no scriptures, no Spiritual Guides.

In the Buddhist scriptures, it is said that if someone knows these effects and yet continues to commit non-virtuous actions, he or she is like someone with perfect eyesight who walks straight off the edge of a cliff! However, it is not enough merely to avoid committing such actions in the future—we also have to purify the negative karma we have accumulated in the past. If we do not purify past negative karma, we will have to experience all these effects in the future, but if we practice purification, we can prevent our negative karma from ripening at all. Out of his great compassion, Buddha taught many methods for purifying negative karma. Within these, one of the most powerful is the practice associated with the *Mahayana*

> *If we practice purification, we can prevent our negative karma from ripening at all.*

Sutra of the Three Superior Heaps. This Sutra, and a short explanation of the practice, can be found in Appendix II of this book, and a detailed explanation can be found in the book *The Bodhisattva Vow*.

Buddha Stainless One

Buddha Bestower of Glory

Buddha Pure One

Our Precious Human Life

As we have seen, it is possible to take rebirth in any one of the six realms, depending on what kind of karma ripens when we die. This time, we have taken rebirth as a human being, and so we now have the opportunity to enjoy all the advantages of a human life. If we contemplate these advantages, we will realize that this life is very precious because it presents us with a unique opportunity for spiritual development. Compared to an animal life, for example, a human life generally provides many advantages, such as good food, shelter, and freedom from predators; but the greatest advantage of being human is the special opportunity we have to develop our mind and thereby to free ourself and others from suffering.

A human life has almost limitless potential, but we will be able to realize this potential only if we first learn to appreciate it. Therefore, we need to reflect again and again on the special opportunity we now have. If we develop a deep appreciation for the preciousness of this life, we will definitely make a determination to use it wisely. Then we will feel that our life has become truly meaningful.

Within our mind, there are eighty-four thousand different delusions, all of which produce mental pain or inner disease. This inner disease has no beginning, and until we abandon our deluded states of mind, it will have no end. If we do not overcome our attachment, for example, it will remain in our mind like an insatiable thirst, constantly giving rise to feelings of dissatisfaction and frustration. Similarly, all the other delusions, such as anger, jealousy, and selfishness, will continue to cause us mental pain whenever they arise within our mind.

Even though we have been suffering from these inner diseases since time without beginning, we now have an opportunity to eradicate them completely. Buddha gave eighty-four thousand different instructions to cure these inner diseases, and unlike other living beings, human beings have the opportunity to receive these instructions and put them into practice. Thus, by relying upon Buddha's teachings, we can use our human life to gradually reduce and eventually eradicate altogether our delusions and all the pain and suffering they give rise to.

Generally, there are three ways in which we can use our precious human life to realize its potential. We can use it to ensure that in future lives we will be born as a human being with all the conditions necessary for a happy and meaningful life; we can use it to attain complete liberation from suffering; or we can use it to attain full enlightenment, or Buddhahood, for the sake of all living beings.

With a human mind, we can understand the existence of past and future lives. This understanding leads us to think beyond the preoccupations of this short life and to consider our welfare in future lives. We are led to the conclusion that if we want a good rebirth in the future, we must create the causes for it now, in this life.

How can we do this? We can create the cause for a human rebirth in our next life by practicing moral discipline in this life, we can create the cause to have an attractive body in that life by practicing patience, and we can create the cause to enjoy abundant wealth and resources by practicing giving. We can create the cause for our wishes to be fulfilled by engaging in virtuous actions with a joyful mind, we can create the cause to have a calm and peaceful mind by practicing meditation, and we can destroy our ignorance and solve all our inner problems by improving our wisdom. We can create the cause to enjoy good health and a long life by protecting life and helping the sick, and we can protect ourself from lower rebirth and ensure that we are reborn as a human being or a god by making offerings, prostrations, and prayers to the Buddhas, Bodhisattvas, and other holy beings. In short, we can use this human life to create the cause for any good conditions we wish to experience in the future.

Non-human beings, such as animals, do not have this opportunity, no matter how skilled they may be at other things. For example, some animals are very clever at hunting and finding food, and birds are very skilled at flying, but animals cannot practice moral discipline or even develop the wish to practice it. All living beings, even worms and insects, can commit negative actions, but only human beings have the opportunity to purify them. For example, if we recite with faith the names of the Thirty-five Confession Buddhas in the *Mahayana Sutra of the Three Superior Heaps*, we can swiftly purify even the heaviest negative karma. This Sutra can be found in Appendix II.

However, even if we are reborn as a human being in the next life, we will still not be free from suffering. All living beings within the six realms experience one problem after another. They have to endure the sufferings of birth, sickness, aging, death, disappointment, frustration, and so on, again and again, in life after life. This cycle of uncontrolled death and rebirth pervaded by suffering is called *samsara*. As human beings, we can understand how we are trapped in samsara, what causes us to take rebirth in samsara, and how we can escape from it. With this understanding, we will naturally develop a wish to escape from samsara and attain permanent freedom from suffering. This wish is called *renunciation*. If with this motivation, we engage in the spiritual practices of moral discipline, concentration, and wisdom that are explained in Part Two of this book, we will eventually eradicate all our delusions and attain complete liberation from samsara and all its problems.

Complete liberation from the delusions and suffering, however, is not the greatest goal we can accomplish with our human life. If we consider the plight of others, we will see that all living beings are trapped in samsara, experiencing terrible suffering in life after life. If we then rely on Buddha's Mahayana teachings, we will be able to develop great compassion for all these suffering beings.

Seeing that the only way we can protect them from suffering is to develop all the skills and qualities of a

If we realize that this precious human life has such great potential, we will feel extremely fortunate.

Buddha, we will make a strong determination to become a Buddha for the sake of all living beings. This special mind is called *bodhichitta*, or the *mind of enlightenment*. Once we develop bodhichitta, we become a Bodhisattva and enter into the Bodhisattva's way of life. The essence of the Bodhisattva's way of life is the practice of the six perfections—the perfections of giving, moral discipline, patience, effort, mental stabilization, and wisdom. These are explained in Part Three of this book. If we practice the six perfections sincerely, eventually we will attain full enlightenment and become a Conqueror Buddha.

Just as Prince Siddhartha used his human life to practice Dharma and attain full enlightenment, we can use our precious human life to do the same. If we realize that this precious human life has such great potential, we will feel extremely fortunate, and we will decide not to waste it on meaningless activities but to extract its essence by practicing pure Dharma.

Buddha Transforming with Purity

Buddha Water Deity   *Buddha God of Water Deities*

What is Meditation?

The heart of Dharma practice is meditation. The purpose of meditation is to make our mind calm and peaceful. If our mind is peaceful, we will be free from worries and mental discomfort, and so we will experience true happiness. But if our mind is not peaceful, we will find it very difficult to be happy, even if we are living in the very best conditions. If we train in meditation, our mind will gradually become more and more peaceful, and we will experience a purer and purer form of happiness. Eventually, we will be able to stay happy all the time, even in the most difficult circumstances.

Usually we find it difficult to control our mind. It seems as if our mind is like a balloon in the wind—blown here and there by external circumstances. If things go well, our mind is happy, but if they go badly, it immediately becomes unhappy. For example, if we get what we want, such as a new possession or a new partner, we become excited and cling to them tightly. However, since we cannot have everything we want, and since we will inevitably be separated from the friends and possessions we currently enjoy, this mental stickiness, or attachment, only causes us pain. On the other hand, if we do not get what we want, or if we lose something we like, we become depressed or irritated. For example, if we are forced to work with a colleague we dislike, we will probably become irritated and feel aggrieved, with the result that we will not be able to work with him or her efficiently and our time at work will become stressful and unrewarding.

Such fluctuations of mood arise because we are too closely involved in the external situation. We are like a child making a sandcastle who is excited when it is first made, but who becomes upset when it is destroyed by the incoming tide. By training in meditation, we create an inner space and clarity that enable us to control our mind regardless of the external circumstances. Gradually we develop mental equilibrium, a balanced mind that is happy all the time, rather than an unbalanced mind that oscillates between the extremes of excitement and depression.

If we train in meditation systematically, we will eventually be able to eradicate from our mind the delusions that are the causes of all our problems and suffering. In this way, we will come to experience a permanent inner peace, known as *liberation* or *nirvana*. Then, day and night in life after life, we will experience only peace and happiness.

Meditation is a method for familiarizing our mind with virtue. It is a mind that analyzes or concentrates on a virtuous object. A virtuous object is one that causes us to develop a peaceful mind when we analyze it or concentrate on it. If we contemplate an object and it causes us to develop an unpeaceful mind, such as anger or attachment, this indicates that for us the object is non-virtuous. There are also many objects that are neither virtuous nor non-virtuous, but neutral.

There are two types of meditation: analytical meditation and placement meditation. Analytical meditation involves contemplating the meaning of a Dharma instruction that we have heard or read. By contemplating such instructions deeply, eventually we reach a definite conclusion or cause a specific virtuous state of mind to arise. This is the object of placement meditation. We then concentrate single-pointedly on this conclusion or virtuous state of mind for as long as possible to become deeply familiar with it. This single-pointed concentration is placement meditation. Often, analytical meditation is called simply *contemplation* and placement meditation simply *meditation*. Placement meditation depends on analytical meditation, and analytical meditation depends on listening to or reading Dharma instructions.

The first stage of meditation is to stop distractions and make our mind clearer and more lucid. This can be accomplished by practicing a simple breathing meditation. We choose a quiet place to meditate and sit in a comfortable position. We can sit in the traditional cross-legged posture or in any other position that is comfortable. If we wish, we can sit in a chair. The most important thing is to keep our back straight to prevent our mind from becoming sluggish or sleepy.

We sit with our eyes partially closed and turn our attention to our breathing. We breathe naturally, preferably through the nostrils, without attempting to control our breath, and we try to become aware of the sensation of the breath as it enters and leaves the nostrils. This sensation is our object of meditation. We should try to concentrate on it to the exclusion of everything else.

At first our mind will be very busy, and we might even feel that the meditation is making our mind busier; but in reality we are just becoming more aware of how busy our mind actually is. There will be a great temptation to follow the different thoughts as they arise, but we should resist this and remain focused single-pointedly on the sensation of the breath. If we discover that our mind has wandered and is following our thoughts, we should immediately return it to the breath. We should repeat this as many times as necessary until the mind settles on the breath.

If we practice patiently in this way, gradually our distracting thoughts will subside and we will experience a sense of inner peace and relaxation. Our mind will feel lucid and spacious and we will feel refreshed. When the sea is rough, sediment is churned up and the water becomes murky, but when the wind dies down the mud gradually settles and the water becomes clear. In a similar way, when the otherwise incessant flow of our distracting thoughts is calmed through concentrating on the breath, our mind becomes unusually lucid and clear. We should stay with this state of mental calm for a while.

Even though breathing meditation is only a preliminary stage of meditation, it can be quite powerful. We can see from this practice that it is possible to experience inner peace and contentment just by controlling the mind, without having to depend at all on external conditions. When the turbulence of distracting thoughts subsides and our mind becomes still, a deep happiness and contentment naturally arise from within. This feeling of contentment and well-being helps us cope with the busyness and difficulties of daily life. So much of the stress and tension we normally experience comes from our mind, and many of the problems we experience, including poor health, are caused or aggravated by this stress. Just by doing breathing meditation for ten or fifteen minutes each day, we will be able to reduce this stress. We will experience a calm, spacious feeling in the mind, and many of our usual problems will disappear. Difficult situations will become easier to deal with, we will naturally feel warm and friendly toward other people, and our relationships with others will gradually improve.

> *When the turbulence of distracting thoughts subsides, a deep happiness and contentment naturally arise from within.*

We should train in this preliminary meditation until we gain some experience of it. However, if we want to attain permanent, unchanging inner peace, and if we want to become completely free from problems and suffering, we need to advance beyond simple breathing meditation to more practical forms of meditation, such as the cycle of twenty-one Lamrim meditations explained in *The New Meditation Handbook*. When we do these meditations, we begin by calming the mind with breathing meditation, and then we proceed to the stages of analytical and placement meditation according to the specific instructions for each meditation. Some of these meditations are now introduced in this book.

$\mathcal{D}$eath

$\mathcal{E}$veryone is aware of the fact that, sooner or later, he or she will die, but for most of us this is just a superficial awareness. Deep down we habitually assume that our death will not occur until some time in the distant future. All the time, in the back of our mind, there is the tacit assumption that we will not die today. Even on the day on which we actually die, we will probably be assuming that we will not die and be making plans for the next day! We live our life as if we were going to remain in this world forever, and consequently, we devote almost all of our time to the affairs of this life and think little about what will happen after we die.

Our preoccupation with trivial, mundane activities causes us to waste our precious human life. Instead of using it to accomplish one of the three great goals mentioned earlier, we use it only to obtain food, clothing, and shelter, to acquire material possessions, to indulge in sex and other superficial pleasures, and to seek promotion and high social status. In this respect, we are no different from animals who scavenge

Buddha Glorious Excellence

Buddha Glorious Sandalwood

Buddha Endless Splendor

for food, make shelters, produce young, protect their territory, and vie for supremacy within the herd or flock.

A human life such as ours is extremely rare and difficult to obtain, so what a great tragedy it would be if, instead of using it to advance spiritually, we were to waste it by living like an animal. The best way to avoid wasting our precious life is to become acutely aware of our impermanence by meditating on death.

We meditate on death to acquaint our mind with three thoughts:

1. I will definitely die.
2. The time of my death is utterly uncertain.
3. At the time of my death and after my death only the practice of Dharma will help me.

We need to meditate on these thoughts again and again in analytical meditation until we develop a deep experience of them and they come to affect the way we live our life. To acquaint ourself with the first thought, we can contemplate three lines of reasoning:

1. I will definitely die because there is no way to prevent my body from finally decaying.
2. Day by day, moment by moment, my life is slipping away.
3. My death will come regardless of whether or not I have made the time to practice Dharma.

By contemplating these points, we come to a clear conclusion, "I will definitely die," and we meditate on this conclusion in placement meditation.

Then we contemplate the following three points:

1. I have no idea when I will die. I may be young and healthy, but this does not mean that I will not die soon. Many young people die before their parents. There is no certainty in this world.
2. There are many causes of untimely death. For example, many strong and healthy people die as a result of unforeseen accidents.
3. This human body is extremely fragile and can easily be destroyed, even by the smallest of objects.

By contemplating these points, we realize that the time of our death is completely uncertain and that we have absolutely no guarantee that we will not die today. When we are convinced of this, we should mentally repeat over and over again, "I may die today, I may die today," and concentrate on the feeling it evokes.

Then we contemplate the following three points:

1. At the time of my death, my wealth and possessions will be of no benefit to me.
2. At the time of my death, my family and friends will not be able to help me.
3. At the time of my death, even my body will be of no use to me.

By contemplating these points, we realize that at the time of our death and after our death only Dharma practice will help us, and we meditate on this conclusion.

Finally, we conclude our contemplations by making three resolutions:

I will practice Dharma.
I will practice Dharma right now.
I will practice Dharma purely.

We meditate on these determinations without distraction for as long as we can. We should put these resolutions into practice and integrate them into our daily life. By doing this, we can protect ourself from the dangers of lower rebirth, attain a permanent cessation of all suffering, and even accomplish full enlightenment.

Buddha Glorious Light

*Buddha Glorious One
without Sorrow*

Buddha Son without Craving

The Buddhist Way of Life

Although we have taken a human rebirth in this life, this does not mean that we will always be a human being. Until we have thoroughly purified our mind, it is quite possible that after we die we will be reborn as an animal, as a hungry spirit, or as a hell being. However, if we rely sincerely on Buddha, Dharma, and Sangha, we will protect ourself from the danger of lower rebirth and from all other dangers.

Buddha, Dharma, and Sangha are called the *Three Jewels* because they are very precious. If we realize the danger we are in, develop complete confidence in the power of the Three Jewels to protect us, and then make a heartfelt determination to rely on the Three Jewels for the rest of our life, at that moment we enter the Buddhist path and become a Buddhist. Once we become a Buddhist, we have the opportunity to accomplish all the spiritual realizations of the Buddhist path, from the realization of relying on a Spiritual Guide through to the Path of No More Learning, or Buddhahood.

From this, we can see that there are two main causes of going for refuge to the Three Jewels: realizing the danger we are in and developing conviction in the power of the Three Jewels to protect us from this danger. To generate the first cause in our mind, we need to become convinced of the possibility of our being reborn as an animal, a hungry spirit, or a hell being. We can do this by considering the following reasoning.

We are blown to the place of our next rebirth by the winds of our karma.

When we die, our mind has to leave this present body, which is just a temporary home, and find another body, rather like a bird leaving one nest to fly to another. Our mind has no freedom to remain and no choice about where to go. We are blown to the place of our next rebirth by the winds of our karma. If the karma that ripens at our death time is negative, we will definitely take a lower rebirth. Heavy negative karma causes rebirth in hell, less negative karma causes rebirth as a hungry spirit, and the least negative karma causes rebirth as an animal.

It is very easy to commit heavy negative karma. For example, simply by swatting a mosquito out of anger we create the cause to be reborn in hell. Throughout this and all our countless previous lives, we have committed many heavy negative actions. Unless we have already purified these actions by practicing sincere confession, their potentialities remain in our mental continuum, and any one of these negative potentialities could ripen when we die. Bearing this in mind, we should think:

If I die today, where will I be tomorrow? It is quite possible that I will find myself in the animal realm, among the hungry spirits, or in hell. If someone were to call me a stupid cow today, I would find it difficult to bear, but what will I do if I actually become a cow, a pig, or a fish?

We should contemplate this until we generate a strong fear of taking rebirth in the lower realms. This fear is the first main cause of going for refuge to the Three Jewels. More reasons establishing the possibility of rebirth in the lower realms can be found in *Joyful Path of Good Fortune*.

To develop the other main cause of going for refuge—a conviction that Buddha, Dharma, and Sangha have complete power to protect living beings from lower rebirth—we should contemplate as follows. The actual refuge is Dharma. As mentioned earlier, Dharma is Buddha's teachings and our own inner experience of these teachings. It is our Dharma, our own spiritual realizations, that directly protects us from taking rebirth in the lower realms. How is this? The cause of lower rebirth is negative actions, which we commit because our mind is under the influence of delusions. By practicing Buddha's teachings, we become familiar with special, virtuous states of mind that are the direct opposite of these delusions. As our virtuous minds become more powerful, our delusions naturally become weaker. For example, as our experience of love increases, our hatred decreases, and as our ability to rejoice in others' good fortune improves, our jealousy diminishes. As our negative minds become weaker, we stop committing the negative karma that causes us to take rebirth in the lower realms. This is how our inner experience of Dharma protects us from the danger of lower rebirth.

If we train in the more advanced Buddhist practices described later in this book, particularly in the wisdom realizing emptiness, eventually we will gain a direct experience of ultimate truth, emptiness, and in this way permanently eradicate all our delusions. Once our mind is completely free from delusions, we will be liberated from all suffering forever.

While Dharma is the actual refuge, Buddha is the source of all refuge. He is the supreme Spiritual Guide who shows us the way to attain Dharma realizations and who sustains our Dharma practice by bestowing his blessings. The Sangha are the supreme spiritual friends who support our Dharma practice. They provide conducive conditions, encourage us in our practice, and set a good example for us to follow. Only the Three Jewels have the ability to protect living beings from all suffering.

If we contemplate these points carefully, we will generate a strong conviction that Buddha, Dharma, and Sangha have complete power to protect living beings from lower rebirth, and from all fear and suffering. This conviction is the second main cause of going for refuge. With these two main causes firmly established in our mind, we should pray every day to the Three Jewels by reciting the following refuge prayer:

All Buddhas, Bodhisattvas, and holy beings,
Please protect me and all living beings
From the various sufferings, fears, and dangers of
*   samsara.*
Please bestow your blessings upon our body and mind.

In this prayer, "Buddhas" refers to the Buddha Jewel, and "Bodhisattvas and holy beings" to the Sangha Jewel, the assembly of Superior beings who have realized ultimate truth directly. When we recite this verse, we imagine that in front of us is the living Buddha Shakyamuni surrounded by all the Buddhas and Bodhisattvas, like the full moon surrounded by stars. We generate a strong conviction that all these holy beings are actually present before us and develop strong faith in them.

When we recite the words, "Please protect me," while concentrating on their meaning, we are familiarizing our mind with renunciation, the wish to release ourself from the various sufferings, fears, and dangers of samsara. When we recite, "and all living beings," we are familiarizing our mind with great compassion, the wish to release all other living beings from these sufferings, fears, and dangers. When we recite the last line, we are requesting the Buddhas, Bodhisattvas, and other holy beings to bless us so that the realizations of renunciation and great compassion will grow within our mind. These realizations are Dharma Jewels.

In summary, by reciting this verse while contemplating its meaning, we are establishing within our mind the special Dharma Jewels of the realizations of renunciation and great compassion by receiving the blessings of the Buddha Jewel and the Sangha Jewel. This is the real meaning of going for refuge to the Three Jewels. If we are able to remember this practice when we die, we will definitely be protected from rebirth in the lower realms.

The foundation of the Buddhist way of life is to go for refuge to the Three Jewels from the depths of our heart every day, and to keep purely the twelve commitments of going for refuge. These are explained in Appendix I. The essential meaning of these commitments is that we should have complete faith and confidence in the Three Jewels and live in accordance with the laws of karma—abandoning non-virtuous actions such as killing and stealing, and practicing virtuous actions such as maintaining a compassionate mind toward human beings and animals alike. Anyone who wishes to follow the Buddhist path should become thoroughly familiar with these twelve commitments.

PART TWO

The Path to Liberation

Buddha Glorious Flower

Buddha Clearly Knowing through Enjoying Pure Radiance

Buddha Clearly Knowing through Enjoying Lotus Radiance

What is Liberation?

Liberation is a permanent inner peace attained through the complete abandonment of delusions. When through training in the paths to liberation, our mind is completely released from delusions, the ultimate nature of our mind becomes a liberation, or a nirvana. From that moment on, we are free from samsara and all its sufferings. We have become a Foe Destroyer, a person who has destroyed the inner enemies of attachment, hatred, and self-grasping ignorance.

As mentioned earlier, forty-nine days after Buddha attained enlightenment he was requested by Brahma and Indra to turn the Wheel of Dharma. The first teaching Buddha gave was the *Sutra of the Four Noble Truths*, in which he explained about true sufferings, true origins, true cessations, and true paths. Samsaric rebirth, such as our present rebirth, is called *true suffering* because it is the basis of all other suffering and delusions. Delusions and actions motivated by delusions are called *true origins* because they are the origin, or source, of all sufferings. Liberation is called a *true cessation* because it is a permanent cessation of delusions and sufferings. The paths that lead to liberation are called *true paths* because by following these paths we attain true cessations. Buddha said:

> You should know sufferings.
> You should abandon origins.
> You should attain cessations.
> You should meditate on paths.

The meaning of this is that we should first understand that samsaric rebirth is the nature of suffering and develop renunciation for it. Then we should abandon the delusions and negative actions that are the source, or origin, of samsaric rebirth and all its sufferings, and make our human life meaningful by attaining liberation. To attain this permanent cessation of suffering, we should practice the paths to liberation.

The four noble truths can be understood and practiced on many different levels. Directly or indirectly, all Dharma practices are included within the practice of the four noble truths. At a basic level, we can begin the practice of the four noble truths by reflecting on the sufferings caused by anger. Anger destroys both peace of mind and peace in the world. The root cause of the two World Wars and of all the wars being fought in various parts of the world today is anger. On a smaller scale, anger destroys our personal relationships, our reputation, and the harmony within families and communities. Most of the arguments and most of the day-to-day difficulties we experience with our family, friends, and colleagues are due to anger. The root of all our future happiness is our virtuous karmic potentialities, the positive energy produced by our past virtuous actions that we carry in our mental continuum. Anger destroys these potentialities and thereby robs us of the good effects of our virtuous actions. In addition, by causing us to commit heavy negative actions, anger can even throw us into the fires of hell in future lives. Nothing harms us more than anger.

Recognizing the terrible and unnecessary sufferings that arise from anger, we should develop renunciation for them and then strive to abandon their cause, the mind of anger, by practicing patience. In this way, we can attain a cessation of anger. The sufferings caused by anger are true sufferings, anger itself is a true origin, the practice of patience is a practice of true paths, and the permanent cessation of anger is a true cessation. We can also apply the same principles to the sufferings caused by attachment and ignorance.

More details on the four noble truths and how to overcome anger can be found in *How to Solve Our Human Problems*.

Buddha Glorious Wealth

Buddha Glorious
Mindfulness

Buddha Glorious Name
of Great Renown

Developing Renunciation

Wherever we are born in samsara, even in the highest god realm, there is no freedom from suffering. Certainly the human realm is not free from suffering. We only have to look around us, read a newspaper, or watch television to see that human beings experience terrible sufferings. In addition, if we succeed in taking rebirth in the fortunate realms, it is only like taking a short vacation. Afterward, we once again have to descend to the lower realms, where we experience extreme suffering for inconceivably long periods. We experience all these sufferings because we are in samsara. If we think deeply about this, we will realize that if we want real freedom and real happiness, we must escape from samsara.

To escape from samsara, we must cut its root by eradicating self-grasping from our mental continuum. This depends on training in higher wisdom, which depends on training in higher concentration, which depends on training in higher moral discipline. These three trainings are called *higher trainings* because they are motivated by renunciation. Therefore our first step in escaping from samsara is to develop renunciation.

We develop renunciation by contemplating the many faults of samsara, such as those described below. We may wonder why it is necessary to contemplate sufferings such as birth, aging, sickness, and death, especially since we have already experienced the first and can do nothing to avoid the others. The

If we want real freedom and real happiness, we must escape from samsara.

reason is that by meditating on these sufferings we realize that the very nature of samsaric existence is suffering, and that until we escape from samsara, we will have to experience the same pains in life after life. This induces a strong wish to escape from samsara by abandoning its cause, self-grasping. This wish is renunciation.

There now follow seven separate contemplations on the sufferings of samsara. It is not necessary to contemplate all these points every time we meditate. Instead we should contemplate mainly those points that have the greatest impact on our mind and that help us to develop renunciation. When a strong feeling of renunciation arises in our mind, we should refrain from further analysis and focus our mind single-pointedly on this feeling for as long as possible.

In these contemplations, we think about the various sufferings experienced in the human realm, but we should bear in mind that the sufferings of other realms are generally far worse.

BIRTH

We have to spend the first nine months of our life cramped inside our mother's womb. At the beginning, the rapid growth of our limbs makes us feel as if we are being stretched out on a rack, and in the later months of pregnancy, we feel as if we are squashed inside a small water tank full of filthy liquid. We are extremely sensitive to everything our mother does. For example, if she runs, our fragile body is severely jolted, and if she drinks anything hot, it feels like boiling water scalding our skin. During all this time, we are completely alone. Our mother does not know the suffering and fear that we experience, and even if she did, she would be powerless to help us.

When we finally emerge from the womb, it is like being forced through a narrow crevice between two hard rocks into a harsh and alien world. We have forgotten everything we knew in our previous life and have no way of understanding what is now happening to us. It is as if we were blind, deaf, and dumb. Our skin is so tender that even the softest clothes feel abrasive. When we are hungry we cannot say, "I need food," and when we are in pain we cannot say, "This is hurting me." The only signs we can make are hot tears and furious gestures. We are completely helpless and have to be taught everything—how to eat, how to sit, how to walk, how to talk.

AGING

As we grow old, our youthful vitality diminishes. We become bent, ugly, and burdened with illness. Our eyesight becomes weaker and our hearing fails. We cannot derive the same enjoyment from the things we used to enjoy, such as eating, drinking, and sex. We are too weak to play games, and we are often too exhausted even for entertainment. When we are young, we can travel around the whole world, but when we are old we can hardly walk to our own front door. We become too weak to engage in many worldly activities, and our spiritual activities are often curtailed. For example, we cannot make many prostrations or travel far to receive teachings. If we meditate, we find it harder to gain realizations because our memory and concentration are weak and we find it difficult to stay awake. Our intellect is less sharp than it was during our youth, and so when we try to study it takes much longer to understand things.

Unable to do the work we used to do, or to help others in the way we would like to, we begin to feel useless to society and start to lose our self-respect. We are often neglected by our own children, and we watch helplessly as one by one our friends and contemporaries grow sick and die. Inexorably, our loneliness deepens. If we did not practice Dharma while we were younger and had the opportunity, we pass our few remaining years with a growing fear of death and a deepening sense of regret for a wasted life.

SICKNESS

Having been born as a human being, it is almost impossible to escape having to experience sickness in this life. When we get sick, we are like a bird that has been soaring in the sky and is suddenly shot down. When a bird is shot, it falls straight to the ground like a lump of lead and all its glory and power are immediately destroyed. Even a mild illness can be completely incapacitating. We cannot enjoy the food we like or take part in the activities of our friends. We may be told that we must never again eat our favorite food, drink alcohol, or engage in strenuous exercise. If our disease is more serious, we may have to undergo painful and possibly risky operations. If these fail, we will be told that the doctors cannot do anything to cure us and that we only have a short time left to live. If we have not used our life to practice Dharma, we will be overcome by fear and regret.

Young people in their prime may be struck down by an incurable degenerative illness, and though they remain alive for many years, they will have to watch themselves slowly deteriorate. Realizing that their most treasured hopes and dreams will never be fulfilled, they may wish they could die sooner. When we hear or read about the horrible diseases experienced by others, we must remember that the same could happen to us. While we remain in samsara, we are never safe from the threat of sickness.

DEATH

If during our life we have worked hard to acquire possessions and have become very attached to them, we will experience great suffering when we are separated from them at the time of death. Even now, we find it difficult to lend one of our most treasured possessions to someone else, let alone to give it away. No wonder we become so miserable when we realize that, in the hands of death, we must abandon everything.

When we die, we are separated from even our closest friends. We have to leave our partner, even though we may have been together for many years and never spent a day apart. If we are very attached to our friends, we will experience great misery at the time of death, but all we will be able to do is to hold their hands. We will not be able to stop the process of death, even if they plead with us not to die. Usually when we are very attached to someone, we feel jealous if he or she leaves us on our own and spends time with someone else, but when we die we will have to leave our friends with others forever. If we have children, we will have to leave them when we die. We will have to leave our spiritual friends and all the people who have helped us in this life.

When we die, this body that we have cherished and cared for in so many ways will have to be left behind. It will become mindless like a stone and will be buried in the ground or cremated. If we have not practiced Dharma and cultivated virtuous actions, at the time of death we will develop fear and distress, as well as bodily pain.

HAVING TO PART WITH WHAT WE LIKE

Before the final separation at the time of death, we often have to experience temporary separation from the people and things we like. We may have to leave our country where all our friends and relatives live, or we may have to leave the job we like. We may lose our reputation. Many times in this life we have to experience the misery of parting from the people we like, or abandoning and losing the things we find pleasant and attractive, but when we die we have to part forever from all the companions and enjoyments of this life.

HAVING TO ENCOUNTER WHAT WE DO NOT LIKE

We are often forced to live or work with people we find unpleasant, such as those who criticize us for no reason, or with those who continually interfere with our wishes. Sometimes we may find ourself in very dangerous situations, such as in a fire or an earthquake, or attacked by a mugger or a rapist. If our country goes to war, we may be called up to fight, or be imprisoned if we refuse. Our homes may be bombed and our relatives killed. Our lives are full of less extreme situations that we find annoying. On vacation it rains, but back in the office the heat is stifling. Our business fails, or we lose our job, or we use up all our savings. We argue with our partner, our children cause us many worries, and old friends suddenly turn against us. Whatever we do, something always seems to go wrong. Even in our Dharma practice, we continually meet obstacles. When we sit down to meditate, we are distracted by outside noise, the telephone rings, or someone comes to see us. Sometimes it seems that even though we have been practicing Dharma for years, our delusions are stronger than ever. Even though we try so hard to be considerate, sometimes our family or our friends become unhappy about our Dharma practice. It is as if we were living in a thorn bush—whenever we adjust ourself to make ourself more comfortable, the thorns only pierce us more deeply. In samsara, aggravation and frustration are the natural state of affairs.

FAILING TO SATISFY OUR DESIRES

We have countless desires. Many cannot be fulfilled at all and others, when fulfilled, do not bring us the satisfaction we hoped for. Many people are unable to satisfy even modest desires for the basic necessities of life, such as adequate food, clothing, shelter, companionship, tolerable work, or a degree of personal freedom. Unfortunately, even if these basic needs are met, our desires do not end there. Soon we need a car, a more luxurious home, a better-paying job. In the past, a simple vacation at the beach may have been sufficient, but our expectations continually increase and now we need expensive vacations in foreign countries.

Ambition and competitiveness are a common cause of dissatisfaction. The ambitious child in school cannot be content until he or she becomes first in the class, nor the businessman until he has made his fortune. Clearly, not everyone can be at the top. For one person to win, others must lose, but even the winners are rarely satisfied for long; their ambition drives them on until they too are beaten, worn out, or dead.

Another reason why we fail to satisfy all our desires is that they are often contradictory. For example, we may want both worldly success and a simple life, or fame and privacy, or rich food and a slim body, or excitement and security. We may demand our own way all the time and still expect to be popular, or we *Samsara promises much but can never deliver real satisfaction.* may wish for Dharma realizations yet still covet a good reputation and material wealth. Our desires often involve other people, and this creates special complications. Many relationships break up because of unrealistic expectations and desires.

We seek perfection—the perfect society, the perfect home, the perfect partner—but perfection cannot be found in samsara. Samsara promises much but can never deliver real satisfaction. It is not possible for impure, transient objects to provide the lasting joy we seek. This can be attained only by thoroughly purifying our mind. Ignorance is the fundamental cause of samsara, but worldly desires are the fuel that perpetuates it; therefore we need to reduce our worldly desires by recognizing their faults.

By contemplating these seven types of suffering, we will come to the following conclusion:

I have experienced these sufferings over and over again in the past, and if I do not attain liberation, I will have to experience them over and over again in the future. Therefore, I must escape from samsara.

When this thought arises clearly and definitely in our mind, we meditate on it for as long as possible.

If we do this meditation again and again, eventually the wish to attain liberation from samsara will arise spontaneously, day and night. At that time, we will have attained the actual realization of renunciation and entered the actual path to liberation. Every action motivated by renunciation is a cause for attaining liberation.

If we have some experience of renunciation, we can transform our everyday activities into the path to liberation by maintaining the intention to benefit others and mentally dedicating the virtue of our actions to our own and others' liberation from samsara. When we meet with difficult circumstances, or see others experiencing difficulties, we should use this to remind ourself of the disadvantages of samsara. When things are going well, we should not be deceived but recall that samsaric pleasures are short-lived and ensnare us if we become attached to them. In this way, we can use all our experiences of daily life to strengthen our determination to escape from samsara and attain liberation.

The Three Higher Trainings

As mentioned before, the actual paths to liberation from samsara are the three higher trainings: higher moral discipline, higher concentration, and higher wisdom. They are called *higher* trainings because they are practiced with the motivation of renunciation. To attain liberation, we need to abandon self-grasping, the root of samsara, by attaining a special wisdom directly realizing emptiness, or selflessness. This attainment depends on a special type of concentration known as *tranquil abiding*, which in turn depends on pure moral discipline. Moral discipline helps to pacify our distractions, the main obstacle to attaining the concentration of tranquil abiding; tranquil abiding makes our mind stable, lucid, and powerful; and wisdom realizing emptiness directly opposes self-grasping ignorance. Therefore, if we practice moral discipline, concentration, and wisdom with the motivation of renunciation, we will definitely be able to destroy our self-grasping and attain liberation from samsara.

TRAINING IN HIGHER MORAL DISCIPLINE

In general, moral discipline is a virtuous mental determination to abandon any fault, or a bodily or verbal action motivated by such a determination. We practice moral discipline whenever we put this determination into practice. If our practice of moral discipline is not motivated by renunciation, it will cause us to attain higher rebirth within samsara, such as rebirth as a human being or a god; but if our practice of moral discipline is motivated by renunciation, it will lead to the attainment of liberation from samsara. This is why moral discipline practiced with the motivation of renunciation is called *higher moral discipline*. Higher moral discipline is an actual path to liberation. The pure practices of the ordination vows, the Bodhisattva vows, and the Tantric vows are all included within training in higher moral discipline, and all are paths to liberation.

TRAINING IN HIGHER CONCENTRATION

Pure concentration is a mind whose nature is to be single-pointedly placed on a virtuous object and whose function is to prevent distraction. Concentration practiced with the motivation of renunciation is higher concentration, and is an actual path to liberation. Whenever we engage in meditation with the motivation of renunciation, we are training in higher concentration.

There are many levels of concentration. To attain a direct realization of emptiness, the ultimate nature of reality, we need the concentration of tranquil abiding. Tranquil abiding is a concentration that possesses a special type of suppleness attained by progressing through nine levels of concentration called the *nine mental abidings*. When we have attained tranquil abiding, our mind is very stable, clear, and powerful, and so it is very easy for us to attain Dharma realizations. A detailed explanation of how to attain tranquil abiding can be found in *Joyful Path of Good Fortune*.

TRAINING IN HIGHER WISDOM

In general, wisdom is a virtuous mind that functions mainly to dispel doubt and confusion by understanding its object thoroughly. Among the many different types of wisdom, the wisdom that realizes emptiness—the ultimate nature of phenomena—is supreme. Whenever we meditate on emptiness with the motivation of renunciation, we are training in higher wisdom. If we train in higher wisdom, eventually our mind will be released from all delusions, including self-grasping ignorance, and we will attain liberation from samsara.

Anyone who practices these three higher trainings is said to be "maintaining Buddhadharma by means of realization." There are two ways to maintain Buddhadharma: by means of scripture and by means of realization. We maintain

Buddhadharma by means of scripture when we listen to, read, or study Dharma, and we maintain Buddhadharma by means of realization when we actually put these instructions into practice and gain realizations.

PART THREE

The Path to Enlightenment

Buddha King of the Victory Banner

*Buddha Glorious One
Complete Subduer*

*Buddha Great
Victor in Battle*

Becoming a Bodhisattva

As already explained, the most meaningful use to which we can put our precious human life is not to attain liberation from suffering for ourself, but to attain great enlightenment, or Buddhahood, for the sake of all living beings. To do this, we must rely on Buddha's Mahayana teachings. First we generate the special motivation of bodhichitta, and then we enter into the Bodhisattva's way of life and engage in the practice of the six perfections, until eventually, by completing this training, we become an enlightened being, a Buddha.

Bodhichitta is a primary mind motivated by great compassion that wishes to attain full enlightenment for the benefit of all living beings. This special mind does not arise naturally but has to be cultivated in meditation for a long time. Eventually, through the force of familiarity, it becomes spontaneous, arising naturally day and night without effort. When this happens, we become a Bodhisattva, a being bound for enlightenment.

If we train in bodhichitta and follow the Bodhisattva's way of life, eventually our mind will be released from both the delusions and the imprints of the delusions. Delusions are called *obstructions to liberation* because they keep us in samsara. The imprints of the delusions are called *obstructions to omniscience* because they prevent us from attaining a direct and simultaneous cognition of all phenomena. When our mind is completely free from both obstructions, the ultimate nature of our mind becomes a full enlightenment, a great liberation, or a great nirvana, and we ourself become a Conqueror Buddha.

> *If we love others, we naturally feel compassion for them.*

The root of bodhichitta is great compassion, an unbiased compassion that wishes to protect all living beings without exception from suffering. We can develop great compassion only if we first develop affectionate love for all living beings. Affectionate love is a mind that feels close to others and holds them dear. If we love others, we naturally feel compassion for them when we become aware of their suffering. Therefore, to become a Bodhisattva, we must first develop affectionate love for all living beings, and then generate great compassion and bodhichitta.

AFFECTIONATE LOVE

Buddha taught that to develop affectionate love for all living beings we should learn to recognize them as our mothers and contemplate their kindness. To do this, we should contemplate as follows. Since it is impossible to find a beginning to our mental continuum, it follows that we have taken countless rebirths in the past. If we have had countless rebirths, we must have had countless mothers. Where are all these mothers now? They are all the living beings alive today.

It is incorrect to reason that our mothers of former lives are no longer our mothers just because a long time has passed since they actually cared for us. If our present mother were to die today, would she cease to be our mother? No. We would still regard her as our mother and pray for her happiness. The same is true of all our previous mothers—they died, yet they remain our mothers. It is only because of the changes in our external appearance that we do not recognize each other.

In our daily life, we see many different living beings, both human and non-human. We regard some as friends, some as enemies, and most as strangers. These distinctions are made by our mistaken minds; they are not verified by valid minds. As a result of the different karmic relationships we have had in the past, some living beings now appear to us to be attractive, some unattractive, and others neither particularly attractive nor unattractive. We tend to assent to these appearances unquestioningly, as if they were really true. We believe that those who now appear pleasant are intrinsically pleasant people, while those we find unattractive are actually unpleasant. This way of thinking is clearly incorrect. If the people we find attractive were intrinsically pleasant, everyone who met them would find them pleasant; and if the people we find unattractive were intrinsically unpleasant, everyone who met them would find them unpleasant; but this is not the case. Therefore, rather than following such mistaken minds, we should regard all living beings as our mothers. Whoever we meet, we should think, "This person is my mother." In this way, we will feel equally warm toward all living beings.

If we regard all living beings as our mothers, we will find it easy to develop pure love and compassion, our everyday relationships will become pure and stable, and we will naturally avoid negative actions such as killing or harming living beings. Since it is so beneficial to regard all living beings as our mothers, we should adopt this way of thinking without hesitation.

Once we have become convinced that all living beings are our mothers, we should then contemplate their kindness. When we were conceived, if our mother had not wanted to keep us in her womb, she could have had an abortion. If she had done so, we would not now have this human life. Through her kindness, she allowed us to stay in her womb, and so we now enjoy a human life and experience all its advantages. When we were a baby, if we had not received her constant care and attention, we would certainly have had an accident and could now be handicapped, crippled, or blind. Fortunately, our mother did not neglect us. Day and night, she gave us her loving care, regarding us as more important than herself. She saved our life many times each day. During the night she allowed her sleep to be interrupted, and during the day she gave up her usual pleasures. She had to leave her job, and when her friends went out to enjoy themselves she had to stay behind. She spent all her money on us, giving us the best food and the best clothes she could afford. She taught us how to eat, how to walk, how to talk. Thinking of our future welfare, she did her best to ensure that we received a good education. Due to her kindness, we are now able to study whatever we choose. It is principally through the kindness of our mother that we now have the opportunity to practice Dharma and eventually to attain enlightenment.

Our day-to-day needs are provided through the kindness of others.

Since there is no one who has not been our mother at some time in our previous lives, and since when we were their child they treated us with the same kindness as our present mother has treated us in this life, all living beings are very kind.

The kindness of living beings is not limited to the times when they have been our mother. All the time, our day-to-day needs are provided through the kindness of others. We brought nothing with us from our former life, yet as soon as we were born we were given a home, food, clothes, and everything we needed—all provided through the kindness of others. Everything we now enjoy has been provided through the generosity of other beings, past or present.

We are able to make use of many things with very little effort on our own part. If we consider facilities such as roads, cars, trains, airplanes, ships, houses, restaurants, hotels, libraries, hospitals, stores, money, and so on, it is clear that many people worked very hard to provide these things. Even though we contribute little or nothing toward the provision of these facilities, they are all available for us to use. This shows the great kindness of others.

Both our general education and our spiritual training are provided by others. All our Dharma realizations, from our very first insights up to our eventual attainment of liberation and enlightenment, will be attained in dependence upon the kindness of others.

If we recognize that all living beings are our mothers and reflect on their kindness, we will develop affectionate love equally for all living beings. Once a woman asked the great Tibetan Teacher, Geshe Potowa, what affectionate love is, and he replied, "What do you feel when you see your own son? You are delighted to see him and he appears pleasant to you. If we regard all beings in the same way, feeling close to them and holding them dear, we have developed affectionate love."

Our own mother may not be very beautiful or wear very elegant clothes, but because we have a good relationship with her, in our eyes she is beautiful. We love her, and if we notice that she is in pain we naturally feel compassion for her. If we have this same tender regard for all other living beings, we have affectionate love. With this affectionate love for all living beings, it is impossible to become jealous of or angry with others. If we improve our awareness of the kindness of others, we will naturally develop this warm heart and tenderness and thereby come to cherish others. Even though others may possess faults, we will see their beauty, just as a mother sees the beauty of her children, no matter what they do.

GREAT COMPASSION

Great compassion is a spontaneous wish to release all living beings from the sufferings of samsara. Once we have developed affectionate love for all living beings, if we then contemplate how they are all trapped in samsara, experiencing one problem after another, we will easily develop compassion for them. Previously it was explained how to develop renunciation for samsara by contemplating seven types of suffering, from the sufferings of birth up to the suffering of failing to satisfy our desires. If we now recall these contemplations and apply them to others, we will realize that all living beings are experiencing unbearable suffering. We should contemplate these sufferings of others until a strong feeling of compassion for all living beings arises in our heart. Then we should meditate on this feeling without distraction.

BODHICHITTA

When we have developed great compassion for all living beings, we should think:

> *I want to liberate all living beings from samsara, but how can I do this? As long as I remain in samsara myself, I have no power to help them. I cannot even solve all my own problems, let alone the problems of all living beings. Only a Buddha has the power to protect all living beings and bestow on them uncontaminated happiness. Therefore, to fulfill my wish to liberate all living beings from suffering, I will become a Buddha.*

We meditate on this thought again and again until it arises spontaneously in our mind, day and night. When this happens, we have developed the actual realization of bodhichitta and have become a Bodhisattva, a son or daughter of the Buddhas. The mere wish to become a Buddha for the benefit of all living beings is called *aspiring bodhichitta*. If we then make a heartfelt promise to engage in the Bodhisattva's way of life by practicing the six perfections, our aspiring bodhichitta will transform into engaging bodhichitta.

The Bodhisattva's Way of Life

We engage in the Bodhisattva's way of life by practicing the six perfections: the perfections of giving, moral discipline, patience, effort, mental stabilization, and wisdom. These are the actual path to Buddhahood. If we wish to become enlightened but do not practice the six perfections, we are like someone who wants to go somewhere but does not actually set out on the journey. Bodhisattvas have two main tasks: to benefit others right now and to attain full enlightenment to be able to benefit all living beings in the future. Both tasks are accomplished through the practice of the six perfections. The six perfections will now be explained in detail.

THE PERFECTION OF GIVING

Giving is a virtuous mental intention to give, or a bodily or verbal action of giving that is motivated by a virtuous state of mind. Giving practiced with bodhichitta motivation is a perfection of giving. There are three types of giving:

1. Giving material things
2. Giving Dharma
3. Giving fearlessness

Giving material things

To practice giving material things, we first contemplate the disadvantages of miserliness and the benefits of giving, and then we engage in the actual practice of giving to others. In the *Condensed Perfection of Wisdom Sutra*, Buddha teaches that miserliness leads to poverty and rebirth as a hungry spirit. Even in this life, miserliness causes us suffering. It is a tight, uncomfortable mind that leads to isolation and unpopularity. Giving, on the other hand, is a joyful mind that leads us to experience wealth and abundant resources in the future.

Wealth acquires meaning only when it is given away or used to benefit others

There is no point in clinging to our possessions, because wealth acquires meaning only when it is given away or used to benefit others. Since without any choice we will have to part with all our possessions when we die, it is better to part with them now and thereby derive some benefit from having owned them. In addition, if at the time of our death we have strong attachment to our possessions, this will prevent us from having a peaceful death, and may even prevent us from taking a fortunate rebirth.

When we go on vacation, we are careful to carry enough money to see us through the whole trip, but it is much more important to ensure that we travel to future lives with enough virtue, or merit, to provide us with all the resources we will need. Our practice of giving is the best insurance against future poverty.

We should give away our possessions only when the time is right; that is, when it would not cause any hindrances to our spiritual practice or endanger our life, and when the person we are giving to will derive great benefit. Otherwise, we should not give away our possessions even if someone asks for them. For example, if we can see that a gift will cause harm to others, we should not offer it. We need to consider all the implications of our action, including how it will affect others besides the person who is to receive the gift. We also need to keep those things that are necessary for our Dharma practice. If we were to give these away, we would be indirectly harming others because we would be creating obstacles to our progress toward enlightenment for their sake.

We should mentally dedicate all our possessions to others, but we should physically give them away only when it is most suitable to do so. This skillful way of thinking is, in itself, a form of giving. For example, charitable organizations do not immediately give away everything that is donated to them but keep a certain amount in reserve for when it is most needed. Even so, while they are holding on to the money, they do not consider it to be their own; they simply think that they are looking after it for others until a need arises. If we view all our possessions in a similar way, we will be practicing giving all the time.

The amount of merit we accumulate through the practice of giving depends on several factors besides the actual value of the gift. One factor is the nature of the recipient. There are three classes of being to whom it is especially meritorious to give: holy beings, such as our Spiritual Guide, Buddhas, and Bodhisattvas; those who have shown us great kindness, such as our parents; and those who are in great need, such as the poor, the sick, and the handicapped. Another important factor is our motivation. It is more meritorious to give a few crumbs to the birds with a motivation of pure compassion than it is to give a diamond ring out of attachment. The best motivation, of course, is bodhichitta. The virtue created by giving with this motivation is limitless.

Giving Dharma

There are many ways to give Dharma. If, with a good motivation, we teach even just one word of Dharma to others, we are giving Dharma. This is much more beneficial than any kind of material gift because material things help others only in this life, while the gift of Dharma helps them in this and all their future lives. There are many other ways in which we can give Dharma—for example, by dedicating our virtue so that all living beings may enjoy peace and happiness, or by whispering mantras into the ears of animals.

Giving fearlessness

To give fearlessness is to protect other living beings from fear or danger. For example, if we rescue someone from a fire or from some other natural disaster, if we protect others from physical violence, or if we save animals and insects who have fallen into water or are trapped, we are practicing giving fearlessness. If we are not able to rescue those in danger, we can still give fearlessness by making prayers and offerings so that they may be released from danger. We can also practice giving fearlessness by praying for others to become free from their delusions, especially the delusion of self-grasping, which is the ultimate source of all fear.

THE PERFECTION OF MORAL DISCIPLINE

Moral discipline is a virtuous mental determination to abandon any fault, or it is a bodily or verbal action motivated by such a determination. Moral discipline practiced with bodhichitta motivation is a perfection of moral discipline. There are three types of moral discipline:

1. The moral discipline of restraint
2. The moral discipline of gathering virtuous Dharmas
3. The moral discipline of benefiting living beings

The moral discipline of restraint

This is the moral discipline of abstaining from non-virtue. To practice this moral discipline, we need to understand the dangers of committing negative actions, make a promise or vow to abandon them, and then keep that promise or vow. Simply failing to commit negative actions unintentionally is not a practice of moral discipline because it is not motivated by a determination to abstain.

Any spiritual discipline that avoids or overcomes either mental faults or negative actions of body or speech is included within the moral discipline of restraint. For example, if we understand the dangers of the ten non-virtuous actions, promise to refrain from them, and keep that promise, we are practicing the moral discipline of restraint.

Sometimes we can take vows by ourself by recognizing the faults of the actions we want to abandon and promising to refrain from them for whatever length of time we can. Even if we promise to refrain from just one negative action for only a short time—for example, if we promise only to abandon killing for just one week—and we keep that promise, we are practicing the moral discipline of restraint. However, as our capacity increases we should gradually extend the duration of our restraint, and also promise to abandon other non-virtuous actions. When we feel we are ready, we can take special vows from a Spiritual Guide, such as refuge vows, ordination vows, Bodhisattva vows, and Tantric vows. The refuge vows, or commitments, are explained in Appendix I of this book, and the Bodhisattva vows are explained in *The Bodhisattva Vow*.

To practice moral discipline, we need to rely on mindfulness, alertness, and conscientiousness. Mindfulness prevents us from forgetting our vows, alertness keeps a check on our mind and warns us if delusions are about to arise, and conscientiousness protects our mind from non-virtue. For example, we may be in a situation, such as a lively party, in which it would be easy to incur the Bodhisattva downfall of praising ourself and scorning others. However, if we practice mindfulness, we will constantly remember that we have promised not to do such things, and there will be no danger of our incurring this downfall out of forgetfulness. Similarly, if we maintain alertness, we will be able to detect delusions such as pride or envy as soon as they begin to arise, and then use conscientiousness to check their development.

When we take the Bodhisattva vows, we must have the intention to keep them continuously until we are enlightened. If we are to fulfill our wish to attain enlightenment quickly for the sake of others, we need to overcome our faults as soon as we can. For a Bodhisattva, the main object to be abandoned is the intention to work solely for one's own sake. Bodhisattvas see clearly the dangers of self-cherishing—thinking oneself to be supremely important—and they realize that it is the principal obstacle to developing bodhichitta and to attaining enlightenment. In the *Condensed Perfection of Wisdom Sutra*,

Buddha says that the moral discipline of a Bodhisattva does not degenerate if he or she enjoys beautiful forms, sounds, tastes, or other objects of the senses, but if a Bodhisattva develops concern for his own welfare, both his moral discipline and his bodhichitta degenerate. If we generate bodhichitta and later think that it would be better to seek only our own liberation, we incur a root Bodhisattva downfall and break our moral discipline of restraint.

With the motivation of bodhichitta, no action can be non-virtuous because bodhichitta eliminates self-cherishing, which is the root of all non-virtuous actions. Even if a Bodhisattva has to kill, this action is not non-virtuous, because it is performed solely for the benefit of all living beings. Although others may condemn them, Bodhisattvas incur no negative karma when they perform such actions because their bodhichitta ensures that all their actions are pure. This is illustrated by an episode from a previous life of Buddha Shakyamuni, while he was still a Bodhisattva. At that time, he was the captain of a ship that was ferrying five hundred merchants on a special voyage. With his clairvoyance, he saw that one of the merchants was planning to kill all the others. Seeing that as a result of this the merchant would be reborn in hell, he generated great compassion for him and for his intended victims. He decided to take upon himself the karma of killing rather than allow all five hundred merchants to suffer and so, with pure bodhichitta motivation, he killed the evil merchant. In this way, he protected that merchant from a hellish rebirth and saved the lives of all the others. As a result of this action of killing, that Bodhisattva made great spiritual progress.

The moral discipline of gathering virtuous Dharmas

We practice this moral discipline when we sincerely practice any virtuous action, such as keeping the Bodhisattva vows purely, practicing the six perfections, making offerings to the Three Jewels, or putting energy into studying, meditating on, or spreading holy Dharma.

The moral discipline of benefiting living beings

This is the moral discipline of helping others in whatever way we can. If we cannot offer practical help to someone, we can at least make prayers for him or her and maintain a continuous intention to give assistance when an opportunity arises. We can understand how to practice this moral discipline by studying the instructions on the last twelve secondary downfalls of the Bodhisattva vows, explained in *The Bodhisattva Vow*.

When we help others, we should be tactful and sensitive. We should try to understand the other person's experience and point of view, and then offer help that is relevant to him, and in such a way that he can accept it. We cannot help others if we attack their values and beliefs or if we ignore their temperament and their personal circumstances. We have to adapt our own behavior so that it suits the other person and makes him or her feel at ease. Instead of imposing our own moral standards on others and judging them if they do not comply, we should simply act in the way that will have the most positive effect. We need both flexibility of mind and flexibility of behavior.

Since Bodhisattvas have great compassion, they do whatever is necessary to help others. In effect, Bodhisattvas will do whatever needs to be done to make someone else happy because when others are happy their minds are more open and receptive to advice and example. If we wish to influence others, we can do so only if we do not antagonize them or make them feel uncomfortable or frightened.

The tact and sensitivity required by a Bodhisattva when helping others is well illustrated by an episode from the life of the great Tibetan Teacher, Geshe Langri Tangpa. A woman who had recently given birth to a baby girl was frightened that she would lose her baby because she had already given birth to one child who had died in infancy. The woman expressed her anxiety to her mother, who told her that children given into the care of Geshe Langri Tangpa would not die. Later, when the little girl became sick, the woman took her to see Geshe Langri Tangpa, but when she arrived, she found him sitting on a throne giving a discourse to a thousand disciples. The woman began to worry that her

> *Since Bodhisattvas have great compassion, they do whatever is necessary to help others.*

child would die before the end of the discourse. She knew that Geshe Langri Tangpa was a Bodhisattva and would show patience, and so she walked up to the throne, and in a loud, affronted tone of voice, declared, "Here, take your baby. Now you take care of her!" She turned to the audience and said, "This is the father of my child," and then turned back to Geshe Langri Tangpa and pleaded softly, "Please don't let her die." Geshe Langri Tangpa just nodded his head in acceptance. As if he really were the father of the child, he wrapped her tenderly in his robes and continued his discourse. His disciples were astonished and asked him, "Are you really the father of that child?" Knowing that if he were to deny it, the woman would have been thought crazy and the people would have ridiculed her, Geshe Langri Tangpa replied that he was.

Although he was a monk, Geshe Langri Tangpa acted like a real father to the child, delighting in her and caring for her. After some time, the mother returned to see how her daughter was doing. When she saw how healthy the child was, she asked Geshe Langri Tangpa if she could have her back again. The Geshe then kindly returned the girl to her mother. When his disciples realized what had happened, they said, "So you're not really the father after all!" and Geshe Langri Tangpa replied, "No, I'm not." In this way, Geshe Langri Tangpa responded to the woman's actions with pure compassion and acted in accordance with the needs of the time.

THE PERFECTION OF PATIENCE

Patience is a virtuous mind that is able to bear harm, suffering, or profound Dharma. Patience practiced with bodhichitta motivation is a perfection of patience.

We need to cultivate patience even if we have no interest in spiritual development, because without it, we remain vulnerable to anxiety, frustration, and disquiet. If we lack patience, it is difficult for us to maintain peaceful relationships with others.

Patience is the opponent to anger, the most potent destroyer of virtue. We can see from our own experience how much suffering arises from anger. It prevents us from judging a situation correctly, and it causes us to act in regrettable ways. It destroys our own peace of mind and disturbs everyone else we meet. Even people who are normally attracted to us are repelled when they see us angry. Anger can make us reject or insult our own parents, and when it is intense, it can even drive us to kill the people we love or even to take our own life.

Usually anger is triggered by something quite insignificant, such as a comment that we take personally, a habit that we find irritating, or an expectation that was not fulfilled. Based on such small experiences, anger weaves an elaborate fantasy, exaggerating the unpleasantness of the situation, and providing rationalizations and justifications for the sense of disappointment, outrage, or resentment. It leads us to say and do harmful things, thereby offending others and transforming a small difficulty into a great problem.

If we were asked, "Who caused all the wars in which so many people have died?" we would have to reply that they were caused by angry minds. If nations were full of calm, peace-loving people, how could wars ever arise? Anger is the greatest enemy of living beings. It harmed us in the past, it harms us now, and if we do not overcome it through the practice of patience, it will continue to harm us in the future. As Shantideva says:

This enemy of anger has no function
Other than to harm me.

External enemies harm us in slower and less subtle ways. If we practice patience with them, we can even win them over and turn them into our friends; but there can be no reconciliation with anger. If we are lenient with anger, it will take advantage of us and harm us even more. In addition, while external enemies can harm us only in this life, anger harms us for many future lives. Therefore, we need to eliminate anger as soon as it enters our mind, because if we do not, it will quickly become a blazing fire that consumes our merit.

Patience, on the other hand, helps us in this life and in all future lives. As Shantideva says:

There is no evil greater than anger,
And no virtue greater than patience.

With patience, we can accept any pain that is inflicted upon us and we can easily endure our usual troubles and inconveniences. With patience, nothing upsets our peace of mind and we do not experience problems. With patience, we maintain an inner peace and tranquility that allows spiritual realizations to grow. Chandrakirti says that if we practice patience we will have a beautiful form in the future, and we will become a holy being with high realizations.

There are three types of patience:

1. The patience of not retaliating
2. The patience of voluntarily enduring suffering
3. The patience of definitely thinking about Dharma

The patience of not retaliating

To practice this type of patience, we need to remain continuously mindful of the dangers of anger and the benefits of patient acceptance, and whenever anger is about to arise in our mind, we need to immediately apply the methods for eliminating it. We begin by learning to accept small difficulties, such as insignificant insults or minor disruptions to our routine, and then gradually improve our patience until we are able to accept even the greatest difficulty without getting angry.

When we are meditating on patience, we can use many different lines of reasoning to help us overcome our tendency to retaliate. For example, we can contemplate that if someone hit us with a stick, we would not get angry with the stick, because it was being wielded by the attacker and had no choice. In the same way, if someone insults us or harms us, we should not get angry with him, because he is being manipulated by his deluded minds and also has no choice. Similarly, we can think that just as a doctor does not get angry if a feverish patient lashes out at him, so we should not get angry if confused living beings, suffering from the sickness of the delusions, harm us in any way. There are many special lines of reasoning such as these to be found in *Joyful Path of Good Fortune*, *Meaningful to Behold* and *How to Solve Our Human Problems*.

The fundamental reason why we receive harm is that we have harmed others in the past. Those who attack us are merely the conditions that ripen our karma; the real cause of all the harm we receive is our own negativity. If in such circumstances we retaliate, we simply create more negative karma and so we will have to suffer even more harm in the future. If we patiently accept injury, however, we break the chain and that particular karmic debt is paid off.

The patience of voluntarily enduring suffering

If we do not have the patience of voluntarily enduring suffering, we become discouraged whenever we encounter obstacles and whenever our wishes go unfulfilled. We find it hard to complete our tasks because we feel like abandoning them as soon as they become difficult, and our miseries are further aggravated by our impatience. However, it is possible to accept and endure pain if we have a good reason to do so, and whenever we practice such patience we actually reduce our sufferings. For example, if someone were to stick a sharp needle into our flesh, we would find the pain unbearable, but if the needle contained a vaccine that we needed, our tolerance would increase considerably.

Even to accomplish worldly goals, people are prepared to endure adversity. Businessmen sacrifice their free time and peace of mind just to make money, and soldiers put up with extreme hardship simply to kill other soldiers. How much more willing should we be to accept difficulties for the sake of the most worthwhile aim of all—the attainment of enlightenment for the benefit of all living beings? Because we are in samsara, we often have to endure unpleasant conditions and misfortune. With the patience of voluntarily enduring suffering, however, we can happily and courageously accept these adversities whenever they arise. When our wishes are not fulfilled, or when we are sick, grieving, or otherwise in difficulty, we should not be discouraged. Instead of feeling self-pity, we should use our suffering to strengthen our spiritual practice. We can recall that all our suffering is the result of our previous negative karma, and resolve to practice pure moral discipline in the future. Or we can contemplate that for as long as we remain in samsara suffering is inevitable, and thereby increase our wish to escape from samsara. Or we can use our own suffering as an illustration of the much greater suffering experienced by other beings, and in this way strengthen our compassion.

If we are able to endure adversities, we will receive great rewards. Our present sufferings will diminish and we will accomplish both our temporary and our ultimate wishes. Therefore, we should not see suffering as an obstacle to our spiritual practice but as an indispensable aid. As Shantideva says:

> Moreover, suffering has many good qualities.
> Through experiencing it, we can dispel pride,
> Develop compassion for those trapped in samsara,
> Abandon non-virtue, and delight in virtue.

The patience of definitely thinking about Dharma

If we listen to, contemplate, or meditate on Dharma with a patient and joyful mind so as to gain a special experience of it, we are practicing the patience of definitely thinking about Dharma. Such patience is important because if our mind is impatient or unhappy when we engage in Dharma practice, this will obstruct our spiritual progress and prevent us from improving our Dharma wisdom. Even if we find some aspects of our Dharma practice difficult, we still need to engage in them with a happy mind.

THE PERFECTION OF EFFORT

Effort is a mind that delights in virtue. Effort practiced with bodhichitta motivation is a perfection of effort. Effort is not something to be practiced separately, but a practice that should accompany all our virtuous activities. We practice effort when we apply ourself enthusiastically to Dharma study or meditation, strive to accomplish Dharma realizations, or put effort into helping others. Applying ourself energetically to non-virtuous or neutral actions, however, is not a practice of effort.

With effort we can attain mundane and supramundane happiness—it enables us to complete those virtuous actions that cause birth in the fortunate realms, as well as those that lead to liberation and enlightenment. With effort, we can purify all our negativities and attain whatever good qualities we wish for. However, without effort, even if our wisdom is sharp we will be unable to complete our spiritual practices.

To generate effort, we need to overcome the three types of laziness: procrastination, attraction to what is meaningless or non-virtuous, and discouragement. Procrastination is a reluctance or unwillingness to put effort into spiritual practice immediately. For example, although we may have an interest in Dharma and intend to practice it, we may feel that we can postpone our practice until some point in the future—after we have had a vacation, when our children have grown up, or when we retire. This is a dangerous attitude because the opportunity to practice Dharma is easily lost. Death can strike at any time. In addition, when we have finished the particular task that is now preventing us from practicing Dharma, we can be certain that another will arise to take its place. Worldly activities are like an old man's beard—though he may shave it off in the morning, it has grown again by the evening. Therefore, we should abandon procrastination and begin to practice Dharma immediately. The best remedy for the laziness of procrastination is to meditate on our precious human life and on death and impermanence.

Most of us are very familiar with the second type of laziness. We give in to it whenever we watch television for hours on end without caring what comes on, when we indulge in prolonged conversations with no purpose, or when we become engrossed in sports or business ventures for their own sake. Activities such as these dissipate the energy we have for practicing Dharma. Though they may seem pleasant, they deceive us—wasting our precious human life and destroying our opportunity to attain real and lasting happiness. To overcome this type of laziness, we need to meditate again and again on the dangers of samsara, remembering that all the entertainments of worldly life are deceptive because in reality they function only to bind us within samsara and cause us even more suffering.

The laziness of discouragement is very common in these

degenerate times. Since we cannot see with our own eyes living examples of enlightened beings, and since our spiritual progress is often much slower than we expect it to be, we may begin to doubt whether Buddhahood is possible, or we may conclude that it must be so rare that there is almost no hope of attaining it. We may also see faults in our Spiritual Guide and in those who are practicing Dharma, and conclude that they have no realizations and that effort put into Dharma practice is wasted. If we find we are becoming discouraged in this way, we need to remember that every appearance to the minds of ordinary beings is mistaken because it is contaminated by ignorance. We can be certain that when, through practicing Dharma sincerely, we eliminate our ignorance and attain pure minds, pure beings such as Buddhas will definitely appear clearly to us.

If we strive to attain higher realizations before we have mastered the basics, we must expect to become discouraged. We need to understand that even the highest realizations have small beginnings, and learn to value the small experiences of Dharma that we have already attained. Perhaps our attitude toward other people is less biased than it used to be, perhaps we are more patient or less arrogant, or perhaps our faith is stronger. These small improvements are the seeds that will eventually grow into higher realizations and we should cherish them accordingly. We should not expect great changes right away. We all have Buddha nature—the potential to attain great enlightenment—and now that we have met perfect instructions on the Mahayana path, if we practice steadily, without becoming discouraged, eventually we will definitely attain enlightenment without having to undergo great hardships. So what reason is there to become discouraged?

There are three types of effort: armor-like effort, which is a strong determination to succeed that we generate at the beginning of a virtuous action; the effort of gathering virtuous Dharmas, which is the actual effort we apply

We should practice gently and constantly, like a great river that flows day and night, year after year.

when we strive to gain Dharma realizations; and the effort of benefiting others, which is the effort we apply when we strive to benefit other living beings.

We need to apply effort in a skillful way. Some people begin their practice with great enthusiasm and then give up when great results do not appear, like a waterfall caused by a sudden storm cascading furiously for a short time and then trickling away to nothing. Our effort should not be like this. At the very beginning of our practice, we should make a firm decision that we will persevere until we attain Buddhahood no matter how long it takes, even if it takes many lives. Then we should practice gently and constantly, like a great river that flows day and night, year after year.

When we are tired we should relax, and resume our effort when we are properly rested. If we try to force ourself beyond our natural capacity, we will only become tense, irritable, or sick. Dharma practice should be a joyful affair. It is said that when we practice Dharma we should be like a child at play. When children are engrossed in their games, they feel completely contented and nothing can distract them.

THE PERFECTION OF MENTAL STABILIZATION

Mental stabilization, or concentration, is a mind whose nature is to be single-pointedly placed on a virtuous object and whose function is to prevent distraction. Any concentration practiced with bodhichitta motivation is a perfection of mental stabilization.

For ordinary beings, concentration functions mainly by means of mental awareness. Our sense awarenesses can behold and remain single-pointedly on their objects, but these are not concentrations. For example, when our eye awareness stares single-pointedly at a candle, or our ear awareness becomes absorbed in a piece of music, we are not practicing concentration. To improve our concentration so that we attain the nine mental abidings and eventually tranquil abiding, it is necessary for our mind to gather within and dwell upon its object single-pointedly. To accomplish this, we must take as our main object of concentration a generic image, or mental image, that appears to the mental awareness. Eventually, through the power of concentration, the generic image is worn away and the object is perceived directly.

There are many benefits from training in concentration. When the mind is stilled by concentration, the delusions subside and the mind becomes extremely lucid. At the moment, our minds are intractable, refusing to cooperate with our virtuous intentions; but concentration melts the tension in our body and mind and makes them supple, comfortable, and easy to work with. It is difficult for a distracted mind to become sufficiently acquainted with its object to induce spontaneous realizations, because it feels as if the mind is *here* and the object *there*. A concentrated mind, however, enters into its object and mixes with it, and as a result, realizations of the stages of the path are quickly attained.

Mental stabilization can be used for either mundane or supramundane purposes. The highest planes within samsara are entered by refining the mind through the practice of concentration. Samsara has three levels: the desire realm, the form realm, and the formless realm. The three lower realms, the human realm, the demi-god realm, and the lowest level of the god realm are all included within the desire realm. The god realm is divided into three levels: the realm of the desire realm gods, the realm of the form realm gods, and the realm of the formless realm gods. The only way to attain rebirth as a form realm god or a formless realm god is to train in mental stabilization.

Once a meditator has attained tranquil abiding he can, if he wishes, go on to attain rebirth in the form and formless realms. He or she begins by contemplating the gross and painful nature of the desire realm and the relative peace, purity, and subtlety of the form realm. Gradually he abandons the delusions of the desire realm—principally sensual desire and all forms of anger—so that in his next life he can be reborn as a god of the form realm. If the meditator continues to refine his mind, he will gradually ascend to progressively more and more subtle levels of concentration until eventually he attains the so-called *concentration of peak of samsara*. With this concentration, he can be reborn in peak of samsara—the highest level of the formless realm and the highest attainment within samsara. Such a rebirth is attained mainly through the force of concentration, without the wisdom realizing emptiness. Some non-Buddhists mistakenly believe this to be a state of liberation, but although at this stage gross delusions have been suppressed, very subtle delusions still have not been eliminated, and so eventually the grosser delusions will arise and once again the meditator will have to descend to lower states.

Only a direct realization of emptiness has the power to cut the continuum of self-grasping, the root of all delusions, and thereby release us from samsara altogether. Therefore, from the beginning, we should train in tranquil abiding with the motivation of renunciation and bodhichitta so that we can overcome self-grasping together with its imprints and attain great liberation.

In earlier times, it was fairly easy to attain tranquil abiding and the form and formless realm absorptions, but these days—as our merit decreases, our delusions grow stronger, and distractions abound—these attainments are much more difficult. Therefore, we need to prepare well, especially by overcoming desirous attachment, and then be willing to practice steadily for a long time before we can attain higher levels of concentration.

In the course of mastering the concentrations of the form and formless realms, we attain clairvoyance and other miracle powers. Although these have little meaning in themselves, they can be used by Bodhisattvas to enhance their ability to help others. For example, although we may have very good intentions, sometimes, through not knowing others' minds, we misjudge a situation and our actions prove to be more of a hindrance than a help. Such problems can be overcome by developing a clairvoyance that knows others' minds. However, we should not strive to attain clairvoyance and miracle powers simply for our own sake. If we have taken Bodhisattva vows, we should have a strong interest in improving our concentration only as a means of fulfilling our wish to benefit others.

THE PERFECTION OF WISDOM

Wisdom is a virtuous mind that functions mainly to dispel doubt and confusion by understanding its object thoroughly. Wisdom that is motivated by bodhichitta is a perfection of wisdom.

Wisdom is not the same as worldly intelligence. It is possible to have great intelligence but little wisdom. For example, people who invent weapons of mass destruction are very clever from a worldly point of view, but they have very little wisdom. Similarly, there are people who know a great many facts and understand complex technical subjects, but who have no idea how to maintain a peaceful mind and lead a virtuous life. Such people may have great intelligence, but they have little wisdom.

Training in mental stabilization is like shielding our mind from the winds of distracting thoughts.

Wisdom is a special type of understanding that induces peace of mind by clearly distinguishing what is virtuous and to be practiced from what is non-virtuous and to be avoided. Wisdom provides our spiritual practice with vision. Without the guidance of wisdom, the other five perfections would be blind and would not be able to lead us to the final destination of Buddhahood.

A direct realization of ultimate truth, emptiness, can be attained only by a wisdom that is conjoined with tranquil abiding. With a wavering mind, we will never perceive a subtle object such as emptiness clearly enough to be able to realize it directly, just as we cannot read a book properly by the light of a flickering candle. Training in mental stabilization is like shielding our mind from the winds of distracting thoughts, while wisdom is like the light of the flame itself. When these two are brought together, we attain a clear and powerful perception of the object.

After attaining tranquil abiding, we should strive to attain a union of tranquil abiding and superior seeing observing emptiness. The nature of superior seeing is wisdom. Just as tranquil abiding is a special and superior kind of concentration, so superior seeing is a superior wisdom arising in dependence upon tranquil abiding. When we have attained tranquil abiding, our concentration cannot be disturbed by conceptual thoughts. It is unshakeable, like a huge mountain that cannot be moved by the wind. With such stable concentration, we can investigate our observed object more thoroughly. Through the power of repeated investigation, eventually we will gain a superior knowledge of the nature of our object of meditation. This wisdom of investigation induces a special mental suppleness. A wisdom that is qualified by such suppleness is superior seeing.

The principal object of superior seeing is emptiness, the ultimate nature of phenomena. Every phenomenon has two natures: a conventional nature and an ultimate nature. Our mind, for example, has various characteristics and functions, such as its clarity and its ability to cognize objects. These are the conventional nature of the mind. Although the mind has these uncommon characteristics that distinguish it from other phenomena, it does not exist from its own side, independent of other objects. The mind's lack of existing from its own side is its ultimate nature, or emptiness. Emptiness will be explained in more detail in the next chapter.

When we first attain superior seeing observing emptiness, our realization of emptiness is still conceptual, but by continuing to meditate on emptiness with the union of tranquil abiding and superior seeing, we can gradually eliminate the generic image until finally we perceive emptiness directly, without even a trace of conceptuality. A wisdom that realizes emptiness directly has the power to eradicate delusions from the mind; therefore, it is a true path that leads to liberation and enlightenment.

Since Bodhisattvas wish to become enlightened as quickly as possible, they have a strong wish to accumulate powerful merit quickly. Therefore, they practice each of the six perfections in conjunction with all the others. For example, when Bodhisattvas practice giving, they do so without self-interest, expecting nothing in return. In this way, they practice in accordance with their Bodhisattva vows and combine the perfection of giving with the perfection of moral discipline. By patiently accepting any hardships involved, and not allowing anger to arise if no gratitude is shown, they combine the perfection of giving with the perfection of patience. By giving joyfully, they combine the perfection of giving with the perfection of effort. By concentrating their minds, thinking, "May the merit of my action of giving enable this person to attain Buddhahood," they combine the perfection of giving with the perfection of mental stabilization. Finally, by realizing that the giver, the gift, and the action of giving all lack inherent existence, they combine the perfection of giving with the perfection of wisdom.

The other perfections can also be practiced in this way, with each perfection being practiced in conjunction with all the others. This is the armor-like skillful action of a Bodhisattva that hastens the completion of the two collections—the collection of merit and the collection of wisdom—that are the causes of the Form Body and the Truth Body of a Buddha, respectively. Because Bodhisattvas perform all their actions with the motivation of bodhichitta, their whole life is filled with the practice of the six perfections.

Buddha Glorious One
Complete Subduer Passed Beyond

Buddha Glorious Array
Illuminating All

Buddha Jewel Lotus
Great Subduer

Ultimate Truth

$\mathcal{U}$ltimate truth is emptiness. Emptiness is not nothingness, but lack of inherent existence. Inherent existence is mistakenly projected onto phenomena by our self-grasping mind. All phenomena naturally appear to our mind to be inherently existent, and without realizing that this appearance is mistaken, we instinctively assent to it and hold phenomena to exist inherently, or truly. This is the fundamental reason why we are in samsara.

There are two stages to realizing emptiness. The first is clearly to identify the way phenomena appear to our mind to be inherently existent, and how we firmly believe in the truth of this appearance. This is called *identifying the object of negation*. If our understanding of emptiness is to be effective, it is essential that we begin with a very clear image of what is to be negated. The second stage is to refute the object of negation; that is, to prove to ourself using various lines of reasoning that the object of negation does not actually exist. In this way, we will come to realize the absence, or non-existence, of the object of negation, which is emptiness.

Because we grasp most strongly at ourself and our body, we should begin by contemplating the emptiness of these two phenomena. We can do this by training in the two meditations explained below: meditation on the emptiness of the I, and meditation on the emptiness of the body.

THE EMPTINESS OF THE I

Identifying the object of negation

Although we grasp at an inherently existent I all the time, even during sleep, it is not easy to identify how it appears to our mind. To identify it clearly, we must begin by allowing it to manifest strongly by contemplating situations in which we have an exaggerated sense of I, such as when we are embarrassed, ashamed, afraid, or indignant. We recall or imagine such a situation and then, without any comment or analysis, try to attain a clear mental image of how the I naturally appears at such times. We have to be patient at this stage because it may take many sessions before we attain a clear image. Eventually we will see that the I appears to be completely solid and real, existing from its own side without depending on the body or the mind. This vividly appearing I is the inherently existent I that we cherish so strongly. It is the I that we defend when we are criticized, and that we are so proud of when we are praised.

Once we have an image of how the I appears in these extreme circumstances, we should try to identify how it appears normally, in less extreme situations. For example, we can observe the I that is now reading this book and try to discover how it appears to our mind. Eventually we will see that, although in this case there is not such an inflated sense of I, nevertheless the I still appears to be inherently existent, existing from its own side without depending on the body or the mind.

Once we have an image of the inherently existent I, we focus on it for a while with single-pointed concentration, and then we proceed to the second stage.

Refuting the object of negation

If the I exists in the way that it appears, it must exist in one of four ways: as the body, as the mind, as the collection of the body and mind, or as something separate from the body and mind; there is no other possibility. We contemplate this carefully until we become convinced that this is the case, and then we proceed to examine each of the four possibilities:

1. If the I is the body, there is no sense in saying "my body," because the possessor and the possessed are identical.

   If the I is the body, there is no rebirth because the I ceases when the body dies.

   If the I and the body are identical, then since we are capable of developing faith, dreaming, solving mathematical puzzles, and so on, it follows that flesh, blood, and bones can do the same.

Since none of this is true, it follows that the I is not the body.

2. If the I is the mind, there is no sense in saying "my mind," because the possessor and the possessed are identical. But usually when we focus on our mind we say "my mind." This clearly indicates that the I is not the mind.

   If the I is the mind, then since each person has many types of mind, such as the six consciousnesses, conceptual minds, and non-conceptual minds, it follows that each person has just as many I's. Since this is absurd, it follows that the I is not the mind.

3. Since the body is not the I and the mind is not the I, the collection of the body and mind cannot be the I. The collection of the body and mind is a collection of things that are not the I, so how can the collection itself be the I? For example, in a herd of cows, none of the animals is a sheep; therefore, the herd itself is not sheep. In the same way, in the collection of the body and mind, neither the body nor the mind is the I; therefore, the collection itself is not the I.

You may find this point difficult to understand, but if you think about it for a long time, with a calm and positive mind, and discuss it with more experienced practitioners, it will gradually become clear to you. You can also consult authentic books on the subject, such as *Heart of Wisdom*.

4. If the I is not the body, not the mind, and not the collection of the body and mind, the only possibility that remains is that it is something separate from the body and mind. If this is the case, we must be able to apprehend the I without either the body or the mind appearing, but if we imagine that our body and our mind were to disappear completely there would be nothing remaining that could be called the I. Therefore, it follows that the I is not separate from the body and mind.

We should imagine that our body gradually dissolves into thin air, and then our mind dissolves, our thoughts scatter with the wind, our feelings, wishes, and awareness melt into nothingness. Is there anything left that is the I? There is nothing. Clearly, the I is not something separate from the body and mind.

We have now examined all four possibilities and have failed to find the I. Since we have already decided that there is no fifth possibility, we must conclude that the truly existent, or inherently existent, I that normally appears so vividly does not exist at all. Where there previously appeared an inherently existent I, there now appears an absence of that I. This absence of an inherently existent I is emptiness, ultimate truth.

We contemplate in this way until there appears to our mind a generic image of the absence of an inherently existent I. This image is our object of placement meditation. We try to become completely familiar with it by concentrating on it single-pointedly for as long as possible.

Because we have grasped at an inherently existent I since beginningless time, and have cherished it more dearly than anything else, the experience of failing to find the I in meditation can be quite shocking at first. Some people develop fear, thinking that they have become completely non-existent. Others feel great joy, as if the source of all their problems is vanishing. Both reactions are good signs and indicate correct meditation. After a while, these initial reactions will subside and our mind will settle into a more balanced state. Then we will be able to meditate on emptiness in a calm, controlled manner.

We should allow our mind to become absorbed in space-like emptiness for as long as possible. It is important to remember that our object is emptiness, the absence of an inherently existent I, not mere nothingness. Occasionally we should check our meditation with alertness. If our mind has wandered to another object, or if we have lost the meaning of emptiness and are focusing on mere nothingness, we should return to the contemplations to bring emptiness clearly to mind once again.

We may wonder, "If there is no truly existent I, then who is meditating? Who will get up from meditation, speak to others, and reply when my name is called?" Though there is nothing within the body and mind, or separate from the body and mind, that is the I, this does not mean that the I does not exist at all. Although the I does not exist in any of the four ways mentioned above, it does exist conventionally. The I is merely a designation imputed by the conceptual mind on the collection of the body and mind. As long as we are satisfied with the mere designation "I," there is no problem. We can think, "I exist," "I am going to town," and so on. The problem arises only when we look for an I other than the mere conceptual imputation, "I." The self-grasping mind grasps at an I that ultimately exists, independent of conceptual imputation, as if there were a "real" I existing behind the label. If such an I existed, we would be able to find it, but we have seen that the I cannot be found upon investigation. The conclusion of our search was a definite non-finding of the I. This unfindability of the I is the emptiness of the I, the ultimate nature of the I. The I that exists as mere imputation is the conventional nature of the I.

THE EMPTINESS OF THE BODY

Identifying the object of negation

The way to meditate on the emptiness of the body is similar to the way we meditate on the emptiness of the I. First we must identify the object of negation.

Normally when we think, "my body," a body that exists from its own side, and is a single entity not depending upon its parts, appears to our mind. Such a body is the object of negation and is non-existent. "Truly existent body," "inherently existent body," and "body that exists from its own side" all have the same meaning, and all are objects of negation.

Refuting the object of negation

If the body exists as it appears, it must exist in one of two ways: as its parts or separate from its parts; there is no third possibility.

If the body is one with its parts, is it the individual parts or the collection of its parts? If it is the individual parts, then is it the hands, the face, the skin, the bones, the flesh, or the internal organs? By checking carefully, "Is the head the body? Is the flesh the body?" and so on, we will easily see that none of the individual parts of the body is the body.

If the body is not its individual parts, is it the collection of its parts? The collection of the parts of the body cannot be the body. Why? The parts of the body are all non-bodies, so how can a collection of non-bodies be a body? The hands, feet, and so forth are all parts of the body, but not the body itself. Even though all these parts are assembled together, this collection remains simply parts; it does not magically transform into the part-possessor, the body.

If the body is not its parts, the only other possibility is that it is separate from its parts; but if all the parts of the body were to disappear, there would be nothing left that could be called the body. We should imagine that all the parts of our body melt into light and disappear. First the skin dissolves, then the flesh, blood, and internal organs, and finally the skeleton melts and vanishes into light. Is there anything left that is our body? There is nothing. There is no body separate from its parts.

We have now exhausted all possibilities. The body is not its parts and it is not separate from its parts. Clearly, the body cannot be found. Where previously there appeared an inherently existent body, there now appears an absence of that body. This absence of an inherently existent body is the emptiness of the body.

Recognizing this absence to be the lack of an inherently existent body, we meditate on it single-pointedly. Once again, we should examine our meditation with alertness to make sure that we are meditating on the emptiness of the body and not on nothingness. If we lose the meaning of emptiness, we should return to the contemplations to restore it.

As with the I, the fact that the body cannot be found upon investigation does not imply that the body does not exist at all. The body does exist, but only as a conventional imputation. In accordance with accepted convention, we can impute "body" to the collection of limbs, trunk, and head. But if we try to pinpoint the body, hoping to find a substantially existent phenomenon to which the word "body" refers, we find no body. This unfindability of the body is the emptiness of the body, the ultimate nature of the body.

Nothing is inherently existent. This applies to mind, Buddha, and even to emptiness itself.

The body that exists as mere imputation is the conventional nature of the body.

Although it is incorrect to assert that the body is identical with the collection of the limbs, trunk, and head, there is no fault in saying that the body is imputed on this collection. Even though the parts of the body are plural, the body is singular. "Body" is simply an imputation made by the mind that imputes it. It does not exist from the object's side. There is no fault in imputing a singular phenomenon to a group of many things. For example, we can impute the singular "forest" to a group of many trees, or "herd" to a group of many cows.

All phenomena exist by way of convention; nothing is inherently existent. This applies to mind, Buddha, and even to emptiness itself. Everything is merely imputed by mind. All phenomena have parts because physical phenomena have physical parts, and non-physical phenomena have various attributes that can be distinguished by thought. Using the same type of reasoning as above, we can realize that any phenomenon is not one of its parts, not the collection of its parts, and not separate from its parts. In this way, we can realize the emptiness of all phenomena.

It is particularly helpful to meditate on the emptiness of objects that arouse in us strong delusions, such as attachment or anger. By analyzing correctly, we will realize that the object we desire, or the object we dislike, does not exist from its own side—its beauty or ugliness, and even its very existence, are imputed by mind. By thinking in this way, we will discover that there is no basis for attachment or anger.

Due to our bad mental habits arising through beginningless familiarity with self-grasping ignorance, whatever appears to our mind appears to exist from its own side. This appearance is utterly mistaken. In fact, phenomena are completely empty of existing from their own side. Phenomena exist only through being imputed by mind. By familiarizing ourself with this truth, we can eradicate self-grasping, the root of all delusions and faults.

During the day, when we are not in meditation we should try to recognize that whatever appears to our mind lacks true existence. In a dream, things appear vividly to the dreamer, but when the dreamer wakes, he or she immediately realizes that the objects that appeared in the dream were just mental appearances that did not exist from their own side. We should view all phenomena in a similar way. Though they appear vividly to our mind, they lack inherent existence.

Buddha King of Mount Meru

Enlightenment

To attain full enlightenment, we need to progress through five stages called the *five Mahayana paths*. These are:

1. The Mahayana path of accumulation
2. The Mahayana path of preparation
3. The Mahayana path of seeing
4. The Mahayana path of meditation
5. The Mahayana Path of No More Learning

They are called *paths* because just as external paths lead to external destinations, so these internal paths lead us to our ultimate spiritual destination, full enlightenment.

Through training in affectionate love, great compassion, and bodhichitta, eventually we reach the point where we are so familiar with bodhichitta that it arises naturally, day and night. When we attain this spontaneous realization of bodhichitta, we become a Bodhisattva and enter the first of the five Mahayana paths, the path of accumulation. Bodhisattvas on the path of accumulation strive to accumulate merit and wisdom by practicing the six perfections.

During the meditation break, they practice mainly the first four perfections to accumulate merit and to benefit others directly. Of the many ways in which Bodhisattvas help others, the most important is by teaching Dharma. By giving Dharma teachings and guiding others along spiritual paths, Bodhisattvas help living beings to attain pure and lasting happiness. This is not something that can be done just by giving material aid.

Toward the end of the path of accumulation, Bodhisattvas attain a special realization called the *concentration of the Dharma continuum*. With this concentration, they can remember all the Dharma they have studied and understood in previous lives, and they never forget anything they learn in this life. They are also able to see directly the Supreme Emanation Bodies of Buddhas and to receive teachings from them.

In the meditation session, Bodhisattvas on the path of accumulation emphasize the perfections of mental stabilization and wisdom. The main task of a Bodhisattva on this path is to develop a union of tranquil abiding and superior seeing observing emptiness. Most Bodhisattvas on the path of accumulation already have an understanding of emptiness, and since it is impossible to develop spontaneous bodhichitta without tranquil abiding, they have necessarily attained tranquil abiding. They now need to combine their understanding of emptiness with their experience of tranquil abiding through repeated analytical and placement meditation on emptiness. Eventually they reach the point where, rather than interfering with the stability of their concentration, analysis actually enhances their concentration. For them, the concentration of tranquil abiding is like clear and still water and the analysis of superior seeing is like a small fish that swims through the water without disturbing its tranquility. The moment a Bodhisattva attains the union of tranquil abiding and superior seeing observing emptiness, he or she advances to the path of preparation.

The path of preparation is so called because the Bodhisattva is now preparing for a direct realization of emptiness. In the meditation break, the Bodhisattva continues to engage in the perfections of giving, moral discipline, patience, and effort to benefit others and to accumulate merit; and in the meditation session, he or she continues to meditate on emptiness. At this stage, the Bodhisattva's meditation on emptiness is still conceptual—that is, emptiness still appears to his or her mind mixed with a generic image. Because of this, he still has dualistic appearance. The goal of the Mahayana path of preparation is to bring the mind and its object, emptiness, closer and closer together until eventually they mix completely, the generic image dissolves, and all dualistic appearances subside into emptiness. This is attained through repeated meditation on emptiness with a union of tranquil abiding and superior seeing.

To eradicate dualistic appearances, Bodhisattvas meditate on the emptiness of the mind and the emptiness of emptiness. By engaging in these profound meditations with the wisdom of superior seeing, they are able to overcome progressively more and more subtle levels of dualistic appearance. Finally, even the most subtle dualistic appearance ceases during meditative equipoise and the mind and emptiness mix, like water mixing with water. At this point, the mind and its object feel the same. Only emptiness is perceived—no other phenomenon, not even the mind, appears. With this attainment, the Bodhisattva becomes a Superior being and advances to the Mahayana path of seeing.

The path of seeing is so called because on this path emptiness is seen directly, without the interference of a generic image. Having seen ultimate truth directly, the Bodhisattva's mind is in perfect accord with reality. Because he or she can no longer be deceived by appearances, the Bodhisattva becomes a perfectly reliable source of refuge, a Sangha Jewel.

On the path of seeing, the Bodhisattva abandons intellectually-formed delusions, which are delusions formed through incorrect reasoning or through adhering to wrong philosophical or religious views. This is because once he has directly seen emptiness, the real nature of phenomena, it is impossible for these delusions ever to arise in his mind again.

At the same time as attaining the Mahayana path of seeing, the Bodhisattva also attains the first of the ten Bodhisattva grounds, called *Very Joyful*. A Bodhisattva on this ground attains many extraordinary qualities. Strong delusions such as anger and jealousy can no longer arise in his or her mind. For example, no matter how much he is provoked, he will never get angry. In addition, at this stage he does not experience any pain, even if someone were to cut his body into pieces. Having realized directly that both he and his body are empty of inherent existence, being merely imputed by conception, he would feel no more pain when his body was cut than he would if he saw a tree being cut. A Bodhisattva on the first ground also possesses special qualities based on the number "one hundred." For example, he or she can see a hundred Buddhas in one instant, look a hundred eons into the past and future, and emanate a hundred bodies simultaneously. These special qualities are explained in *Ocean of Nectar*.

On each of the ten grounds, the Bodhisattva attains a special experience of one of the perfections. On the first ground, he or she attains a surpassing realization of the perfection of giving. If it benefited living beings, he could give away his body and his life without the slightest regret. On the second ground, he attains a surpassing realization of the perfection of moral discipline and does not commit a single negative action, even in his dreams. On the third ground, he attains a surpassing realization of the perfection of patience, and on the fourth, fifth, and sixth grounds, he attains surpassing realizations of the perfections of effort, mental stabilization, and wisdom, respectively. On the seventh, eighth, ninth, and tenth grounds, the Bodhisattva attains special experiences of the perfections of skillful means, prayer, power, and exalted wisdom, all of which are aspects of the perfection of wisdom.

Although a Bodhisattva on the path of seeing abandons intellectually-formed delusions, he or she cannot yet abandon innate delusions. These are the delusions we are born with, as opposed to those we acquire through exposure to incorrect systems of thought. Since they are very deeply ingrained in our mind, they are more difficult to abandon than intellectually-formed delusions.

When his or her meditation on emptiness becomes powerful enough to abandon the grossest level of innate delusions, the Bodhisattva advances to the path of meditation. There are nine levels of innate delusion—from big-big to small-small. Purifying our mind of these delusions is similar to washing dirty clothes. If our clothes are very dirty, we need to wash them several times before they become completely clean. The worst dirt comes off in the first wash, but to remove the more subtle and ingrained stains, we may have to wash our clothes several times. In the same way, we cannot cleanse our mind of delusions all at once. To purify our mind completely, we need to meditate on emptiness again and again. First we abandon the grossest delusions, and then we gradually abandon more and more subtle levels of delusion.

On the seventh ground, the Bodhisattva develops a wisdom powerful enough to abandon the subtlest delusions, the small-small delusions. And on the eighth ground he has completely abandoned all delusions, including the small-small delusions. However, the Bodhisattva still has the imprints of the delusions, which remain in his or her mind like the way the smell of garlic remains in a container after the garlic itself has been removed. As mentioned before, the imprints of the delusions are the obstructions to omniscience. The Bodhisattva on the eighth ground meditates on emptiness to abandon gross obstructions to omniscience. When he has abandoned these completely, he advances to the ninth ground. On the ninth ground, he continues to meditate on emptiness to abandon the subtle obstructions to omniscience, and when these are completely abandoned, he advances to the tenth ground.

At the very end of the tenth ground, the Bodhisattva enters a meditative equipoise on emptiness called the *vajra-like concentration of the path of meditation*, which acts as the direct antidote to the very subtle obstructions to omniscience. This concentration is also known as the *exalted wisdom of the final continuum* because it is the last mind of a limited being. In the next moment, he or she has abandoned the very subtle obstructions to omniscience and very subtle dualistic appearances, and has attained the Mahayana Path of No More Learning and become a Conqueror Buddha.

It is impossible to describe all the good qualities of a Buddha. A Buddha's compassion, wisdom, and power are completely beyond conception. With nothing left to obscure his mind, he sees all phenomena throughout the universe as clearly as he sees a jewel held in the palm of his hand. Through the force of his or her compassion, a Buddha spontaneously does whatever is appropriate to benefit others. He has no need to think about what is the best way to help living beings—he naturally and effortlessly acts in the most beneficial way. Just as the sun does not need to motivate itself to radiate light and heat, but does so simply because light and heat are its very nature, so a Buddha does not need to motivate himself to benefit others, but does so simply because being beneficial is his very nature.

Buddhas can emanate in any form whatsoever to help living beings.

Like the reflections of the moon that effortlessly appear in any body of still water, a Buddha's emanations spontaneously appear wherever living beings' minds are capable of perceiving them. Buddhas can emanate in any form whatsoever to help living beings. Sometimes they manifest as Buddhists and sometimes as non-Buddhists. They can manifest as women or men, royalty or beggars, law-abiding citizens or criminals. They can even manifest as animals, as wind or rain, or as mountains or islands. Unless we are a Buddha ourself, we cannot possibly say who or what is an emanation of a Buddha.

Of all the ways in which a Buddha helps living beings, the supreme way is by emanating as a Spiritual Guide. Through his or her teachings and immaculate example, an authentic Spiritual Guide leads his or her disciples along the spiritual path to liberation and enlightenment. If we meet a qualified Mahayana Spiritual Guide and put into practice everything he or she teaches, we will definitely attain full enlightenment and become a Conqueror Buddha. We will then be in a position to repay the kindness of all living beings by liberating them from the sufferings of samsara and leading them to the supreme bliss of Buddhahood.

Dedication

$\mathcal{I}$ have written this book, *Introduction to Buddhism*, with a pure motivation. Through the virtue I have collected by composing this book, and through all the other virtues of myself and others, may pure Buddhadharma flourish throughout this world. May all mother beings be released from the prison of samsara as quickly as possible, and may they attain the supreme happiness of a Conqueror Buddha.

Geshe Kelsang Gyatso,
Manjushri Kadampa
Meditation Center

Buddha's Enlightenment Day,
June 1992

APPENDIX I

The Commitments of Going for Refuge

The Commitments of Going for Refuge

When we go for refuge, we make a determination to observe twelve special commitments. By observing these sincerely, we protect our mind of refuge and it gradually becomes more powerful. These commitments lay the foundation for all the realizations of the stages of the path. Realizing this, we should not regard them as a burden, but practice them joyfully and sincerely.

Within the twelve commitments, there are six specific commitments and six general commitments. The six specific commitments are so called because they are related specifically to each of the Three Jewels. There are two commitments related to Buddha, two related to Dharma, and two related to Sangha. In each case, there is one thing to abandon and one thing to practice. The remaining six commitments apply equally to Buddha, Dharma, and Sangha. These twelve commitments will now be briefly explained.

THE TWO COMMITMENTS SPECIFICALLY
RELATED TO BUDDHA

1. Not to go for refuge to teachers who contradict Buddha's view, or to samsaric gods. By going for refuge to Buddha, we have a commitment to abandon going for ultimate refuge to teachers who contradict Buddha's view, or to worldly gods. This does not mean that we cannot receive help from others; it means that we do not rely on others to provide ultimate protection from suffering.

2. To regard any image of Buddha as an actual Buddha. By going for refuge to Buddha, we also have a commitment to regard any image of Buddha as an actual Buddha. Whenever we see a statue of Buddha, whether it is made of gold or anything else, we should see it as an actual Buddha. We should disregard the material or the quality of the craftsmanship, and pay homage by making offerings and prostrations and by going for refuge. If we practice like this, our merit will increase abundantly.

THE TWO COMMITMENTS SPECIFICALLY
RELATED TO DHARMA

3. Not to harm others. By going for refuge to Dharma, we have a commitment to abandon harming others. Instead of treating others badly, we should try, with the best motivation, to benefit them whenever we can. We first need to concentrate on reducing harmful thoughts and generating a beneficial intention toward those who are close to us, such as our friends and family. When we have developed a good heart toward these people, we can gradually extend our practice to include more and more people until, finally, we have a good heart toward all living beings. If we can abandon harmful thoughts and always have a beneficial intention, we will easily attain the realizations of great love and great compassion. In this way, we begin to increase our compassion, which is the very essence of Buddhadharma, from the very beginning of our practice of going for refuge.

4. To regard all Dharma scriptures as the actual Dharma Jewel. By going for refuge to Dharma, we also have a commitment to regard all Dharma scriptures as the actual Dharma Jewel. Dharma is the source of all health and happiness. Since we cannot see actual Dharma Jewels with our eyes, we need to regard Dharma texts as actual Dharma Jewels. Actual Dharma Jewels arise only as a result of learning, contemplating, and meditating on the meaning of the scriptures. We need to respect every letter of the scriptures and every letter of explanation of Buddha's teaching. Therefore, we must treat Dharma books with great care and avoid walking over them or putting them in inappropriate places where they might be damaged or misused. Each time we neglect or mishandle our Dharma books, we create the cause to become more ignorant because these actions are similar to the action of abandoning Dharma. Once the great Tibetan Teacher Geshe Sharawa saw some people playing carelessly with their Dharma books and he said to them, "You should not do that. You already have enough ignorance. Why do you want to make yourselves even more ignorant?"

THE TWO COMMITMENTS SPECIFICALLY RELATED TO SANGHA

5. Not to allow ourself to be influenced by people who reject Buddha's teaching. By going for refuge to Sangha, we have a commitment to stop being influenced by people who reject Buddha's teaching. This does not mean that we should abandon these people, just that we should not let their views influence our mind. Without abandoning love and consideration for others, we need to be vigilant and make sure that we are not being misled by their bad habits and unsound advice.

6. To regard anyone who wears the robes of an ordained person as an actual Sangha Jewel. By going for refuge to Sangha, we also have a commitment to acknowledge anyone who wears the robes of an ordained person as an actual Sangha Jewel. Even if ordained Sangha are poor, we still need to pay respect to them because they are keeping moral discipline and this is something very rare and precious.

THE SIX GENERAL COMMITMENTS

7. To go for refuge to the Three Jewels again and again, remembering their good qualities and the differences between them. Dharma is like a boat that can carry us across the ocean of samsara, Buddha is like the skillful navigator of the boat, and the Sangha are like the crew. Remembering this, we should go for refuge again and again to the Three Jewels.

8. To offer the first portion of whatever we eat and drink to the Three Jewels, while remembering their kindness. Since we need to eat and drink several times each day, if we always offer the first portion of our food or drink to the Three Jewels, remembering their kindness, we will greatly increase our merit. We can do this with the following prayer:

I make this offering to you, Buddha Shakyamuni,
Whose mind is the synthesis of all Buddha Jewels,
Whose speech is the synthesis of all Dharma Jewels,
Whose body is the synthesis of all Sangha Jewels.
O Blessed One, please accept this and bless my mind.

OM AH HUM   *(3x)*

It is important to always remember Buddha's kindness. All our happiness is a result of Buddha's kindness because all Buddha's actions are pervaded by compassion and concern for others, and it is these actions that enable us to perform virtuous actions that are the cause of our happiness.

Without Buddha's kindness, we would not know the real causes of happiness or the real causes of suffering. Buddha taught us how all happiness and suffering depend on the mind. He showed us how to abandon those states of mind that cause suffering and cultivate those states of mind that cause happiness. In other words, he taught us perfect methods for overcoming suffering and attaining happiness. No one else taught us these methods. How kind Buddha is!

Our own human body is proof of Buddha's kindness. It is by virtue of Buddha's blessings and instructions that we were able to create the cause to take rebirth in a human form, with all the freedoms and endowments necessary for spiritual practice. If we are now able to learn Dharma and meet Spiritual Guides, it is only through Buddha's kindness. We can now practice the methods that lead to full enlightenment and gain spiritual realizations only because Buddha was kind enough to turn the Wheel of Dharma and show his example in this world. Even the small wisdom we possess to discriminate between what is beneficial and what is harmful, and to identify Buddha's teaching as worthwhile, is a result of Buddha's kindness.

We should not think that Buddha helps only those who follow him. Buddha attained enlightenment to benefit all living beings. He manifests in many different forms, sometimes even as non-Buddhist teachers, to help others. There is no living being who has not benefited from the kindness of Buddha.

9. With compassion, always to encourage others to go for refuge. We should always try to help others go for refuge, but we should do so skillfully. If we know someone who is interested in Dharma, we should help him or her develop the causes of going for refuge: fear of suffering and faith in the Three Jewels. We can talk to him or her about impermanence—how the conditions of this life change and how our body will grow old and decay—and we can talk about the sufferings of aging, sickness, and death. We can talk about what will happen after death, about the different types of rebirth, and about how all types of rebirth are in the nature of suffering. If we skillfully introduce these things into our conversations, the other person will begin to lose his complacency, and when he starts to feel uneasy, he will naturally want to find out what can be done. At this point, we can explain about Buddha, Dharma, and Sangha, and how they can help us. Then we can explain how to go for refuge.

If we help someone else tactfully in this way, without being arrogant or impatient, we will bring him or her real benefit. It is never certain that the material gifts we give to others will actually help them; sometimes they even cause more problems. The best way to help others is to lead them into Dharma. If we cannot give elaborate explanations, we can at least give appropriate advice to those who are unhappy, and help them to solve their problems by means of Dharma.

10. To go for refuge at least three times during the day and three times during the night, remembering the benefits of going for refuge. So that we never forget the Three Jewels, we should go for refuge once every four hours, or at least three times during the day and three times during

153

the night. If we never forget the Three Jewels, and regularly contemplate the benefits of going for refuge, we will gain realizations very quickly. We should be like a businessman who never forgets his projects even while he is relaxing.

11. To perform every action with complete trust in the Three Jewels. We should rely on the Three Jewels in everything that we do. In this way, all our actions will be successful. There is no need to seek the inspiration and blessings of worldly gods, but we should always try to receive the blessings of Buddha, Dharma, and Sangha by making offerings and requests.

12. Never to forsake the Three Jewels even at the cost of our life, or as a joke. We should never abandon the Three Jewels, because going for refuge is the foundation of all Dharma realizations. Once a Buddhist was taken captive and his enemy said to him, "Give up your refuge in Buddha or I'll kill you." He refused to forsake his refuge and was killed, but when clairvoyants looked, they saw that he had immediately been reborn as a god.

Liberating Prayer
PRAISE TO BUDDHA SHAKYAMUNI

and

Mahayana Sutra of the Three Superior Heaps

Liberating Prayer

PRAISE TO BUDDHA SHAKYAMUNI

O Blessed One, Shakyamuni Buddha,
Precious treasury of compassion,
Bestower of supreme inner peace,

You, who love all beings without exception,
Are the source of happiness and goodness;
And you guide us to the liberating path.

Your body is a wishfulfilling jewel,
Your speech is supreme, purifying nectar,
And your mind is refuge for all living beings.

With folded hands I turn to you,
Supreme unchanging friend,
I request from the depths of my heart:

Please give me the light of your wisdom
To dispel the darkness of my mind
And to heal my mental continuum.

Please nourish me with your goodness,
That I in turn may nourish all beings
With an unceasing banquet of delight.

Through your compassionate intention,
Your blessings and virtuous deeds,
And my strong wish to rely upon you,

May all suffering quickly cease
And all happiness and joy be fulfilled;
And may holy Dharma flourish for evermore.

*Colophon: This prayer was composed by Venerable Geshe Kelsang Gyatso.
It is recited regularly at the beginning of sadhanas in Kadampa Buddhist
Centers throughout the world.*

Mahayana Sutra of the Three Superior Heaps

INTRODUCTION

One of the most powerful methods for purifying negative karma is the practice associated with the *Mahayana Sutra of the Three Superior Heaps*, otherwise known as *The Bodhisattva's Confession of Moral Downfalls*.

There now follows the root text of the Sutra and a short explanation of the practice. A more detailed explanation of this practice can be found in the book *The Bodhisattva Vow*.

Mahayana Sutra of the Three Superior Heaps

Namo: The Bodhisattva's Confession of Moral Downfalls

I, whose name is . . . , at all times go for refuge to the Guru, go for refuge to the Buddha, go for refuge to the Dharma, go for refuge to the Sangha.

To the Teacher, Blessed One, Tathagata, Foe Destroyer, Completely Perfect Buddha, Glorious Conqueror Shakyamuni I prostrate.

To the Tathagata Complete Subduer with the Essence of Vajra I prostrate.

To the Tathagata Jewel of Radiant Light I prostrate.

To the Tathagata Powerful King of the Nagas I prostrate.

To the Tathagata Leader of the Heroes I prostrate.

To the Tathagata Glorious Pleasure I prostrate.

To the Tathagata Jewel Fire I prostrate.

To the Tathagata Jewel Moonlight I prostrate.

To the Tathagata Meaningful to Behold I prostrate.

To the Tathagata Jewel Moon I prostrate.

To the Tathagata Stainless One I prostrate.

To the Tathagata Bestower of Glory I prostrate.

To the Tathagata Pure One I prostrate.

To the Tathagata Transforming with Purity I prostrate.

To the Tathagata Water Deity I prostrate.

To the Tathagata God of Water Deities I prostrate.

To the Tathagata Glorious Excellence I prostrate.

To the Tathagata Glorious Sandalwood I prostrate.

To the Tathagata Endless Splendor I prostrate.

To the Tathagata Glorious Light I prostrate.

To the Tathagata Glorious One without Sorrow I prostrate.

To the Tathagata Son without Craving I prostrate.

To the Tathagata Glorious Flower I prostrate.

To the Tathagata Clearly Knowing through Enjoying Pure Radiance I prostrate.

To the Tathagata Clearly Knowing through Enjoying Lotus Radiance I prostrate.

To the Tathagata Glorious Wealth I prostrate.

To the Tathagata Glorious Mindfulness I prostrate.

To the Tathagata Glorious Name of Great Renown I prostrate.

To the Tathagata King of the Victory Banner, Head of the Powerful Ones I prostrate.

To the Tathagata Glorious One Complete Subduer I prostrate.

To the Tathagata Great Victor in Battle I prostrate.

To the Tathagata Glorious One Complete Subduer Passed Beyond I prostrate.

To the Tathagata Glorious Array Illuminating All I prostrate.

To the Tathagata Jewel Lotus Great Subduer I prostrate.

To the Tathagata Foe Destroyer, Completely Perfect Buddha, King of Mount Meru Seated Firmly on a Jewel and a Lotus I prostrate.

O All you [Tathagatas] and all the others, however many Tathagatas, the Foe Destroyers, the Completely Perfect Buddhas, the Blessed Ones there are dwelling and abiding in all the worldly realms of the ten directions, all you Buddhas, the Blessed Ones, please listen to me.

In this life and in all my lives since beginningless time, in all my places of rebirth while wandering in samsara, I have done negative actions, have ordered them to be done, and have rejoiced in their being done. I have stolen the property of the bases of offering, the property of the Sangha, and the property of the Sanghas of the ten directions, have ordered it to be stolen, and have rejoiced in it being stolen. I have committed the five unbounded heinous actions, have ordered them to be committed, and have rejoiced in their being committed. I have completely engaged in the paths of the ten non-virtuous actions, have ordered others to engage in them, and have rejoiced in their engaging in them.

Being obstructed by such karmic obstructions, I shall become a hell being, or I shall be born as an animal, or I shall go to the land of the hungry spirits, or I shall be born as a barbarian in an irreligious country, or I shall be born as a long-life god, or I shall come to have incomplete senses, or I shall come to hold wrong views, or I shall have no opportunity to please a Buddha.

All such karmic obstructions I declare in the presence of the Buddhas, the Blessed Ones, who have become exalted wisdom, who have become "eyes," who have become witnesses, who have become valid, who see with their wisdom. I confess without concealing or hiding anything, and from now on I will avoid and refrain from such actions.

All you Buddhas, the Blessed Ones, please listen to me. In this life and in all my previous lives since beginningless time, in all my places of rebirth while wandering in samsara, whatever root of virtue there is in my giving to others, even in my giving a morsel of food to one born as an animal; whatever root of virtue there is in my maintaining moral discipline; whatever root of virtue there is in my actions conducive to great liberation; whatever root of virtue there is in my acting to fully ripen sentient beings; whatever root of virtue there is in my generating a supreme mind of enlightenment; and whatever root of virtue there is in my unsurpassed exalted wisdom; all of these assembled, gathered, and collected together, by fully dedicating them to the unsurpassed, to that of which there is no higher, to that which is even higher than the high, and to that which surpasses the unsurpassed, I fully dedicate to the unsurpassed, perfect, complete enlightenment.

Just as the Buddhas, the Blessed Ones of the past, have dedicated fully, just as the Buddhas, the Blessed Ones who are yet to come, will dedicate fully, and just as the Buddhas, the Blessed Ones who are living now, dedicate fully, so too do I dedicate fully.

I confess individually all negative actions. I rejoice in all merit. I beseech and request all the Buddhas. May I attain the holy, supreme, unsurpassed, exalted wisdom.

Whoever are the Conquerors, the supreme beings living now, those of the past, and likewise those who are yet to come, with a boundless ocean of praise for all your good qualities, and with my palms pressed together I go close to you for refuge.

This concludes the Mahayana Sutra entitled *Sutra of the Three Superior Heaps*.

❧

AN EXPLANATION OF THE PRACTICE

This Sutra is called the *Sutra of the Three Superior Heaps* because it contains three "heaps," or collections, of virtue: prostration, purification, and dedication. In this practice, we visualize the Thirty-five Confession Buddhas and practice purification in their presence. In general, all Buddhas have the power to protect living beings from suffering and negative karma. However, because of the prayers and dedications they made while they were Bodhisattvas, these Thirty-five Buddhas have a special karmic link with the human beings of this world. Through the power of their blessings and prayers, we can swiftly purify even the heaviest negative actions simply by faithfully reciting their names.

To increase our enthusiasm for purification practices, and our faith and respect for the Buddhas, we can contemplate as follows:

All of the problems I have experienced since beginningless time, and all of the problems I will experience in the future, result from my negative karma. Therefore, nothing can be more beneficial than to practice purification sincerely.

Buddhas are perfect witnesses to confession. Through the power of their blessings, it is possible to purify all the negative karma I have accumulated since beginningless time. This opportunity to engage in purification is solely due to the kindness of the Buddhas.

In the space in front of us, we visualize Buddha Shakyamuni seated on a jeweled throne supported by eight white elephants, which symbolize the power of purification. In front of Buddha are the remaining thirty-four Buddhas, who are seated in five rows. In the first row, closest to Buddha Shakyamuni, are the first six Buddhas, arranged from left to right as we look at them. In front of these, the remaining twenty-eight Buddhas are arranged in four rows of seven, each row in front of and slightly lower than the preceding one. All these Buddhas sit on jeweled thrones on cushions of a lotus, a moon, and a sun. This assembly of Thirty-five Confession Buddhas is surrounded by all the Buddhas and Bodhisattvas of the ten directions.

We should know the name of each Buddha, as well as the world over which he presides, his color, his hand gestures, the objects that he holds, and the particular negative karma that is purified by reciting his name. The hand gestures and the objects held by each Buddha can be learned by studying the line illustrations in this book. The remaining features can be found in *The Bodhisattva Vow*.

Focusing our mind on the visualized assembly of Thirty-five Buddhas, and recognizing them as the essence of all Buddha Jewels, Dharma Jewels, and Sangha Jewels, we generate deep faith and go for refuge while reciting the opening lines from the Sutra. Then, with the strong faith and conviction we developed by going for refuge, we make physical prostrations while reciting the name of each Buddha as a request for them to purify our negative karma.

There are three ways to make physical prostrations. We can make full-length prostrations by prostrating our whole body on the ground, make half-length prostrations by kneeling respectfully and touching our palms and our forehead to the ground, or make a gesture of respect, such as pressing our palms together at our heart.

We can make one prostration to each Buddha as we recite his name, and then repeat the cycle as many times as we wish. Alternatively, we can make a number of prostrations, say seven, twenty-one, fifty, or a hundred, to the first Buddha while reciting his name, and then go on to make the same number of prostrations to the second Buddha, and so on. If we do this, we will probably not be able to complete the prostrations to all the Thirty-five Buddhas in one session, in which case we simply begin the next session where we left off.

After reciting the names of the Buddhas together with making prostrations, we can either continue to prostrate, or sit down while we recite the rest of the Sutra. We ask the holy beings to give us their attention and witness our confession. We acknowledge that in the past we have committed many heavy negative actions, and with great remorse confess them all in the presence of the holy beings. We generate strong regret by contemplating the fate that awaits us if we fail to purify these actions, and we then practice a special method for purifying them. At our heart, we visualize all the potentials of our negative actions in the form of a black letter PAM. We then imagine that the negative karma of all other living beings gathers in the aspect of smoke and dissolves into the PAM, and we think that the PAM has become the essence of all our own and others' negativity. We imagine that white wisdom lights and nectars descend from the hearts of all the Thirty-five Buddhas and enter our body through the crown of our head. When these lights and nectars reach the PAM, they completely destroy it, just as a light destroys darkness as soon as it is switched on. We firmly believe that all our negative karma created since beginningless time has been purified. The wisdom lights pervade our body and mind—increasing our life span, our good fortune, our physical and mental power, and our Dharma realizations.

We conclude our purification by making a promise to avoid and refrain from negative actions in the future. Some practitioners can promise to refrain from every downfall and negative action for the rest of their lives, and by relying on mindfulness, conscientiousness, and alertness, never break this promise. If we are not yet able to make such a promise, we should first promise to refrain from all negative actions for one week, for example, and then gradually extend the duration of our restraint to a month, a year, and so on, until we can promise to refrain for the rest of our life. It is important to keep whatever promises we have made to the Buddhas and to our Spiritual Guide because broken promises are serious obstacles to our spiritual progress.

After purifying, we practice dedication so that our practice will definitely produce great and powerful results in the future. We begin by requesting the Buddhas to witness our dedication. We then dedicate all of our own and others' virtues to the attainment of a Buddha's Form Body and a Buddha's Truth Body, so that we will be able to benefit all living beings.

We conclude the recitation of the Sutra with a brief prayer of confession, rejoicing, beseeching the Buddhas not to pass away, and requesting them to turn the Wheel of Dharma. The virtues of this short prayer are dedicated to the attainment of the holy, supreme, unsurpassed, exalted wisdom—in other words, Buddha's omniscient wisdom.

The last lines of the Sutra explicitly teach refuge in the Buddhas of the three times and implicitly reveal refuge in Dharma and Sangha. The essential meaning of these lines is that the practice of the three superior heaps—prostration, purification, and dedication—should be combined with refuge in the Three Jewels.

The best way to avoid committing negative actions or incurring downfalls is always to maintain a good heart through the practice of the twenty-one meditations explained in *The New Meditation Handbook*. The best method for purifying negative actions and downfalls already accumulated is to practice the *Sutra of the Three Superior Heaps*. With these two practices, we will be able to safeguard our entire Bodhisattva's way of life.

Glossary

Alertness A mental factor that is a type of wisdom that examines our activity of body, speech, and mind and knows whether or not faults are developing. See *Understanding the Mind*.

Aspiring bodhichitta A bodhichitta that is a mere wish to attain enlightenment for the benefit of all living beings. See also *Bodhichitta*.

Attachment A deluded mental factor that observes its contaminated object, regards it as a cause of happiness, and wishes for it. See *Understanding the Mind*.

Avalokiteshvara The embodiment of the compassion of all the Buddhas. Called *Chenrezig* in Tibetan. See *Living Meaningfully, Dying Joyfully*.

Bardo See *Intermediate state*.

Blessing The transformation of our mind from a negative state to a positive state, from an unhappy state to a happy state, or from a state of weakness to a state of strength, through the inspiration of holy beings such as our Spiritual Guide, Buddhas, and Bodhisattvas.

Bodhichitta A Sanskrit term for "mind of enlightenment." *Bodhi* means "enlightenment," and *chitta* means "mind." There are two types of bodhichitta—conventional bodhichitta and ultimate bodhichitta. Generally speaking, the term *bodhichitta* refers to conventional bodhichitta, which is a primary mind motivated by great compassion that spontaneously seeks enlightenment to benefit all living beings. There are two types of conventional bodhichitta—aspiring bodhichitta and engaging bodhichitta. Ultimate bodhichitta is a wisdom motivated by conventional bodhichitta that directly realizes emptiness, the ultimate nature of phenomena. See also *Aspiring bodhichitta* and *Engaging bodhichitta*. See *Joyful Path of Good Fortune*.

Bodhisattva A person who has generated spontaneous bodhichitta but who has not yet become a Buddha. From the moment a practitioner generates a non-artificial, or spontaneous, bodhichitta, he or she becomes a Bodhisattva and enters the first Mahayana path, the path of accumulation. An ordinary Bodhisattva is one who has not realized emptiness directly, and a Superior Bodhisattva is one who has attained a direct realization of emptiness. See *Joyful Path of Good Fortune* and *Meaningful to Behold*.

Brahma A worldly god, who resides in the first form realm. See *Ocean of Nectar*.

Buddha A being who has completely abandoned all delusions and their imprints. Every living being has the potential to become a Buddha. See *Joyful Path of Good Fortune*.

Buddhadharma See *Dharma*.

Buddha nature The root mind of a living being, and its ultimate nature. Buddha nature, Buddha seed, and Buddha lineage are synonyms. All living beings have Buddha nature and therefore the potential to attain Buddhahood. See *Mahamudra Tantra*.

Buddha's bodies A Buddha has four bodies—the Wisdom Truth Body, the Nature Body, the Enjoyment Body, and the Emanation Body. The first is Buddha's omniscient mind. The second is the emptiness, or ultimate nature, of his or her mind. The third is his subtle Form Body. The fourth, of which each Buddha manifests a countless number, are gross Form Bodies that are visible to ordinary beings. The Wisdom Truth Body and the Nature Body are both included within the Truth Body, and the Enjoyment Body and the Emanation Body are both included within the Form Body. See *Joyful Path of Good Fortune* and *Ocean of Nectar.*

Buddha Shakyamuni The fourth of one thousand founding Buddhas who are to appear in this world during this Fortunate Eon. The first three were Krakuchchanda, Kanakamuni, and Kashyapa. The fifth Buddha will be Maitreya.

Central channel The principal channel at the very center of the body, along which the channel wheels are located. See *Clear Light of Bliss* and *Mahamudra Tantra*.

Channel wheel Called chakra in Sanskrit. A focal center where secondary channels branch out from the central channel. Meditating on these points can cause the inner winds to enter the central channel. See *Mahamudra Tantra* and *Tantric Grounds and Paths*.

Clairvoyance Abilities that arise from special concentration. There are five principal types of clairvoyance: the clairvoyance of divine eye (the ability to see subtle and distant forms), the clairvoyance of divine ear (the ability to hear subtle and distant sounds), the clairvoyance of miracle powers (the ability to emanate various forms by mind), the clairvoyance of knowing previous lives, and the clairvoyance of knowing others' minds. Some beings, such as bardo beings and some human beings and spirits, have contaminated clairvoyance that is developed due to karma, but these are not actual clairvoyance.

Clear light A manifest very subtle mind that perceives an appearance like clear, empty space. See *Clear Light of Bliss* and *Mahamudra Tantra*.

Collection of merit A virtuous action motivated by bodhichitta that is a main cause of attaining the Form Body of a Buddha. Examples are making offerings and prostrations to holy beings with bodhichitta motivation, and the practice of the perfections of giving, moral discipline, and patience.

Collection of wisdom A virtuous mental action motivated by bodhichitta that is a main cause of attaining the Truth Body of a Buddha. Examples are listening to, contemplating, and meditating on emptiness with bodhichitta motivation.

Conceptual mind A thought that apprehends its object through a generic, or mental, image. See *Understanding the Mind*.

Confession Purification of negative karma by means of the four opponent powers—the power of reliance, the power of regret, the power of the opponent force, and the power of promise. See *The Bodhisattva Vow*.

Conscientiousness A mental factor that, in dependence upon effort, cherishes what is virtuous and guards the mind from delusion and non-virtue. See *Meaningful to Behold* and *Understanding the Mind*.

Contentment Being satisfied with one's inner and outer conditions, motivated by a virtuous intention.

Conventional nature See *Ultimate nature.*

Dedication Dedication is by nature a virtuous mental factor; it is the virtuous intention that functions both to prevent accumulated virtue from degenerating and to cause its increase. See *Joyful Path of Good Fortune.*

Degenerate times A period when spiritual activity degenerates.

Delusion A mental factor that arises from inappropriate attention and functions to make the mind unpeaceful and uncontrolled. There are three main delusions: ignorance, desirous attachment, and anger. From these all the other delusions arise, such as jealousy, pride, and deluded doubt. See also *Innate delusions* and *Intellectually-formed delusions.* See *Joyful Path of Good Fortune* and *Understanding the Mind.*

Demon (*Mara* in Sanskrit.) Anything that obstructs the attainment of liberation or enlightenment. There are four principal types of demon: the demon of the delusions, the demon of contaminated aggregates, the demon of uncontrolled death, and the Devaputra demons. Of these, only the last are actual living beings. The principal Devaputra demon is wrathful Ishvara, the highest of the desire realm gods, who inhabits Land of Controlling Emanations. Buddha is called a *Conqueror* because he or she has conquered all four types of demon. See *Heart of Wisdom.*

Desire realm The environment of hell beings, hungry spirits, animals, human beings, demi-gods, and the gods who enjoy the five objects of desire.

Dharma Buddha's teachings and the inner realizations that are attained in dependence upon practicing them. *Dharma* means "protection." By practicing Buddha's teachings, we protect ourself from suffering and problems.

Dharmapala A manifestation of a Buddha or Bodhisattva, whose main function is to eliminate obstacles and gather all necessary conditions for pure Dharma practitioners. Also called *Dharma Protector*. See *Heart Jewel*.

Dualistic appearance The appearance to mind of an object together with the inherent existence of that object. See *Heart of Wisdom*.

Emptiness Lack of inherent existence, the ultimate nature of phenomena. See *Transform Your Life* and *Heart of Wisdom*.

Engaging bodhichitta After we have taken the Bodhisattva vow, our aspiring bodhichitta transforms into engaging bodhichitta, which is a mind that actually engages in the practices that lead to enlightenment. See also *Bodhichitta*.

Exalted wisdom A spiritual realization that knows perfectly the nature of its principal object. Sometimes called *exalted awareness*. See also *Path/Spiritual path*.

Faith A naturally virtuous mind that functions mainly to oppose the perception of faults in its observed object. There are three types of faith: believing faith, admiring faith, and wishing faith. See *Transform Your Life* and *Understanding the Mind*.

Foe Destroyer (*Arhat* in Sanskrit.) A practitioner who has abandoned all delusions and their seeds by training on the spiritual paths, and who will never again be reborn in samsara. In this context, the term *Foe* refers to the delusions.

Form Body The Enjoyment Body and the Emanation Body of a Buddha. See also *Buddha's bodies*. See *Joyful Path of Good Fortune*.

Form realm The environment of the gods who possess form and who are superior to desire realm gods. So called because the gods who inhabit it have subtle form.

Formless realm The environment of the gods who do not possess form.

Four noble truths True sufferings, true origins, true cessations, and true paths. They are called *noble* truths because they are supreme objects of meditation. Through meditation on these four objects, we can realize ultimate truth directly and thus become a noble, or Superior, being. Sometimes referred to as the *four truths of Superiors*. See *Joyful Path of Good Fortune* and *How to Solve Our Human Problems*.

Generic image The appearing object of a conceptual mind. See *Understanding the Mind*.

Geshe A title given by Kadampa monasteries to accomplished Buddhist scholars. A contracted form of the Tibetan *ge wai she nyen*, literally meaning "virtuous friend."

God (*Deva* in Sanskrit.) A being of the god realm, the highest of the six realms of samsara. There are many different types of god. Some are desire realm gods, while others are form or formless realm gods. See *Joyful Path of Good Fortune*.

Great liberation Great enlightenment, or Buddhahood.

Ground/Spiritual ground A clear realization that acts as the foundation of many good qualities. A clear realization is a realization held by spontaneous renunciation or bodhichitta. The ten grounds are the realizations of Superior Bodhisattvas. See also *Path/Spiritual path*. See *Ocean of Nectar*.

Hinayana (A Sanskrit term for "Lesser Vehicle".) The Hinayana goal is to attain merely one's own liberation from suffering by completely abandoning delusions. See *Joyful Path of Good Fortune*.

Imprint There are two types of imprint: imprints of actions and imprints of delusions. Every action we perform leaves an imprint on the mental consciousness, and these imprints are karmic potentialities to experience certain effects in the future. The imprints left by delusions remain even after the delusions themselves have been abandoned, like the way the smell of garlic lingers in a container after the garlic has been removed. Imprints of delusions are obstructions to omniscience, and are completely abandoned only by Buddhas.

Imputation, mere According to the highest school of Buddhist philosophy, the Madhyamika-Prasangika school, all phenomena are merely imputed by conception in dependence upon their basis of imputation. Therefore, they are mere imputations and do not exist from their own side at all. See *Transform Your Life* and *Heart of Wisdom*.

Indra A worldly god. See *Heart of Wisdom*.

Innate delusions Delusions that are not the product of intellectual speculation, but that arise naturally. See *Understanding the Mind*.

Inner winds Special subtle winds related to the mind that flow through the channels of our body. Our body and mind cannot function without these winds. See *Mahamudra Tantra* and *Tantric Grounds and Paths*.

Intellectually-formed delusions Delusions that arise as a result of relying on incorrect reasoning or mistaken tenets. See *Understanding the Mind.*

Intention A mental factor that functions to move its primary mind to the object. It functions to engage the mind with virtuous, non-virtuous, and neutral objects. All bodily and verbal actions are initiated by the mental factor intention. See *Understanding the Mind.*

Intermediate state (*Bardo* in Tibetan.) The state between death and rebirth. It begins the moment the consciousness leaves the body, and ceases the moment the consciousness enters the body of the next life. See *Joyful Path of Good Fortune.*

Jealousy A deluded mental factor that feels displeasure when observing others' enjoyments, good qualities, or good fortune. See *Understanding the Mind.*

Je Tsongkhapa (AD 1357-1419) An emanation of the Wisdom Buddha Manjushri, whose appearance in fourteenth-century Tibet as a monk, and the holder of the lineage of pure view and pure deeds, was prophesied by Buddha. He spread a very pure Buddhadharma throughout Tibet, showing how to combine the practices of Sutra and Tantra, and how to practice pure Dharma during degenerate times. His tradition later became known as the *Gelug,* or *Ganden Tradition.* See *Heart Jewel* and *Great Treasury of Merit.*

Kadampa A Tibetan word in which *Ka* means "word" and refers to all Buddha's teachings, *dam* refers to Atisha's special Lamrim instructions known as the "stages of the path to enlightenment," and *pa* refers to a follower of Kadampa Buddhism who integrates all the teachings of Buddha that they know into their Lamrim practice. See also *Kadampa Buddhism* and *Kadampa Tradition.*

Kadampa Buddhism A Mahayana Buddhist school founded by the great Indian Buddhist Master Atisha (AD 982-1054). See also *Kadampa* and *Kadampa Tradition*.

Kadampa Tradition The pure tradition of Buddhism established by Atisha. Followers of this tradition up to the time of Je Tsongkhapa are known as *Old Kadampas*, and those after the time of Je Tsongkhapa are known as *New Kadampas*. See also *Kadampa*, *Kadampa Buddhism*, and *New Kadampa Tradition*.

Lamrim A Tibetan term, literally meaning "stages of the path." A special arrangement of all Buddha's teachings that is easy to understand and put into practice. It reveals all the stages of the path to enlightenment. For a full commentary, see *Joyful Path of Good Fortune*.

Land of the Thirty-three Heavens One of the six abodes of desire realm gods. These are, in sequence: Land of the Four Great Kings, Land of the Thirty-three Heavens, Land without Combat, Joyful Land, Land of Enjoying Emanations, and Land of Controlling Emanations.

Langri Tangpa, Geshe (AD 1054-1123) A great Kadampa Teacher who was famous for his realization of exchanging self with others. He composed *Eight Verses of Training the Mind*. See *Eight Steps to Happiness*.

Living being Any being who possesses a mind that is contaminated by delusions or their imprints. Both *living being* and *sentient being* are terms used to distinguish beings whose minds are contaminated by either of these two obstructions from Buddhas, whose minds are completely free from these obstructions.

Maitreya The embodiment of the loving kindness of all the Buddhas. At the time of Buddha Shakyamuni, he manifested as a Bodhisattva disciple in order to show Buddha's disciples how to be perfect Mahayana disciples. In the future, he will manifest as the fifth founding Buddha.

Mantra A Sanskrit word, literally meaning "mind protection." Mantra protects the mind from ordinary appearances and conceptions. There are four types of mantra: mantras that are mind, mantras that are inner wind, mantras that are sound, and mantras that are form. In general, there are three types of mantra recitation: verbal recitation, mental recitation, and vajra recitation. See *Tantric Grounds and Paths*.

Mara See *Demon*.

Meditative equipoise Single-pointed concentration on a virtuous object such as emptiness. See *Ocean of Nectar*.

Mental awareness All minds are included within the five sense awarenesses and mental awareness. There are two types of mental awareness: conceptual mental awarenesses and non-conceptual mental awarenesses. Conceptual mental awareness and conceptual mind are synonyms. See *Understanding the Mind*.

Mental factor A cognizer that principally apprehends a particular attribute of an object. There are fifty-one specific mental factors. Each moment of mind comprises a primary mind and various mental factors. See *Understanding the Mind*.

Mental suppleness A flexibility of mind induced by virtuous concentration. See *Understanding the Mind*.

Merit The good fortune created by virtuous actions. It is the potential power to increase our good qualities and produce happiness.

Mindfulness A mental factor that functions not to forget the object realized by the primary mind. See *Understanding the Mind* and *Meaningful to Behold*.

Miracle powers See *Clairvoyance*.

Nagarjuna A great Indian Buddhist scholar and meditation master who revived the Mahayana in the first century AD by bringing to light the teachings on the *Perfection of Wisdom Sutras*. See *Ocean of Nectar*.

New Kadampa Tradition—International Kadampa Buddhist Union (NKT-IKBU) The union of Kadampa Buddhist Centers, an international association of study and meditation centers that follow the pure tradition of Mahayana Buddhism derived from the Buddhist meditators and scholars Atisha and Je Tsongkhapa, introduced into the West by the Buddhist teacher Venerable Geshe Kelsang Gyatso.

Nine mental abidings Nine levels of concentration leading to tranquil abiding: placing the mind, continual placement, re-placement, close placement, controlling, pacifying, completely pacifying, single-pointedness, and placement in equipoise. See *Joyful Path of Good Fortune*.

Non-conceptual mind A cognizer to which its object appears clearly without being mixed with a generic image. See *Understanding the Mind*.

Object of negation An object explicitly negated by a mind realizing a negative phenomenon. In meditation on emptiness, or lack of inherent existence, it refers to inherent existence. Also known as *negated object*. See *Heart of Wisdom*.

Ordinary being Anyone who has not realized emptiness directly.

Path/Spiritual path An exalted awareness conjoined with non-fabricated, or spontaneous, renunciation. Spiritual path, spiritual ground, spiritual vehicle, and exalted awareness are synonyms. See also *Ground/Spiritual Ground*. See *Ocean of Nectar*.

Perfection of Wisdom Sutras Sutras of the second turning of the Wheel of Dharma, in which Buddha revealed his final view of the ultimate nature of all phenomena—emptiness of inherent existence. See *Heart of Wisdom*.

Primary mind A cognizer that principally apprehends the mere entity of an object. Synonymous with consciousness. There are six primary minds: eye consciousness, ear consciousness, nose consciousness, tongue consciousness, body consciousness, and mental consciousness. Each moment of mind comprises a primary mind and various mental factors. A primary mind and its accompanying mental factors are the same entity but have different functions. See *Understanding the Mind*.

Prostration An action of showing respect with body, speech, or mind. See *Joyful Path of Good Fortune* and *The Bodhisattva Vow*.

Puja A ceremony in which offerings and other acts of devotion are performed in front of holy beings.

Pure Land A pure environment in which there are no true sufferings. There are many Pure Lands. For example, Tushita is the Pure Land of Buddha Maitreya, Sukhavati is the Pure Land of Buddha Amitabha, and Dakini Land (or Keajra) is the Pure Land of Buddha Vajrayogini and Buddha Heruka. See *Living Meaningfully, Dying Joyfully*.

Purification Generally, any practice that leads to the attainment of a pure body, speech, or mind. More specifically, a practice for purifying negative karma by means of the four opponent powers. See *Joyful Path of Good Fortune* and *The Bodhisattva Vow.*

Realization A stable and non-mistaken experience of a virtuous object that directly protects us from suffering.

Sangha According to the Vinaya tradition, any community of four or more fully ordained monks or nuns. In general, ordained or lay people who take Bodhisattva vows or Tantric vows can also be said to be Sangha.

Secret Mantra Synonymous with Tantra. Secret Mantra teachings are distinguished from Sutra teachings in that they reveal methods for training the mind by bringing the future result, or Buddhahood, into the present path. Secret Mantra is the supreme path to full enlightenment. The term *Mantra* indicates that it is Buddha's special instruction for protecting our mind from ordinary appearances and conceptions. Practitioners of Secret Mantra overcome ordinary appearances and conceptions by visualizing their body, environment, enjoyments, and deeds as those of a Buddha. The term *Secret* indicates that the practices are to be done in private, and that they can be practiced only by those who have received a Tantric empowerment. See *Mahamudra Tantra.*

Self-cherishing A mental attitude that considers oneself to be supremely important and precious. It is regarded as a principal object to be abandoned by Bodhisattvas. See *Eight Steps to Happiness.*

Self-grasping A conceptual mind that holds any phenomenon to be inherently existent. The mind of self-grasping gives rise to all other delusions, such as anger and attachment. It is the root cause of all suffering and dissatisfaction. See *Heart of Wisdom.*

Sense awareness All minds are included within sense awareness and mental awareness. There are five types of sense awareness: eye awareness, ear awareness, nose awareness, tongue awareness, and body awareness. See *Understanding the Mind*.

Shantideva (AD 687-763) A great Indian Buddhist scholar and meditation master. He composed *Guide to the Bodhisattva's Way of Life*. See *Meaningful to Behold* and *Guide to the Bodhisattva's Way of Life*.

Spiritual Guide (*Guru* in Sanskrit, and *Lama* in Tibetan.) A Teacher who guides us along the spiritual path. See *Joyful Path of Good Fortune* and *Great Treasury of Merit*.

Stages of the path See *Lamrim*.

Superior being (*Arya* in Sanskrit.) A being who has a direct realization of emptiness. There are Hinayana Superiors and Mahayana Superiors.

Superior seeing A special wisdom that sees its object clearly, and that is maintained by tranquil abiding and the special suppleness that is induced by investigation. See *Joyful Path of Good Fortune*.

Suppleness See *Mental suppleness*.

Supreme Emanation Body A special Emanation Body displaying the thirty-two major signs and eighty minor indications that can be seen by ordinary beings only if they have very pure karma. See also *Buddha's bodies*.

Sutra The teachings of Buddha that are open to everyone to practice without the need for an empowerment. These include Buddha's teachings of the three turnings of the Wheel of Dharma.

Tantra See *Secret Mantra*.

Ten directions The four cardinal directions, the four intermediate directions, and the directions above and below.

Three Jewels The three objects of refuge: Buddha Jewel, Dharma Jewel, and Sangha Jewel. They are called *Jewels* because they are both rare and precious. See *Joyful Path of Good Fortune*.

Tranquil abiding A concentration that possesses the special bliss of physical and mental suppleness that is attained in dependence upon completing the nine mental abidings. See *Joyful Path of Good Fortune* and *Meaningful to Behold*.

Transference of consciousness (*Powa* in Tibetan.) A practice for transferring the consciousness to a Pure Land at the time of death. See *Living Meaningfully, Dying Joyfully*.

Truth Body (*Dharmakaya* in Sanskrit.) The Nature Body and the Wisdom Truth Body of a Buddha. See also *Buddha's bodies*.

Ultimate nature All phenomena have two natures—a conventional nature and an ultimate nature. In the case of a table, for example, the table itself, and its shape, color, and so forth are all the conventional nature of the table. The ultimate nature of the table is the table's lack of inherent existence. The conventional nature of a phenomenon is a conventional truth, and its ultimate nature is an ultimate truth. See *Heart of Wisdom*.

Vajra-like concentration The last moment of the Mahayana path of meditation. It is the antidote to the very subtle obstructions to omniscience. In the next moment, one attains the Mahayana Path of No More Learning, or Buddhahood.

Valid cognizer/mind A cognizer that is non-deceptive with

respect to its engaged object. There are two types: inferential valid cognizers and direct valid cognizers. See *Heart of Wisdom* and *Understanding the Mind.*

Vehicle/Spiritual vehicle An exalted awareness that leads to one's final spiritual destination. See also *Path/Spiritual path.*

Vow A virtuous determination to abandon particular faults that is generated in conjunction with a traditional ritual. The three sets of vows are the Pratimoksha vows of individual liberation, the Bodhisattva vows, and the Secret Mantra or Tantric vows. See *The Bodhisattva Vow.*

NKT – IKBU

Study Programs of Kadampa Buddhism

*K*adampa Buddhism is a Mahayana Buddhist school founded by the great Indian Buddhist Master Atisha (AD 982-1054). His followers are known as *Kadampas*. *Ka* means "word" and refers to Buddha's teachings, and *dam* refers to Atisha's special Lamrim instructions known as "the stages of the path to enlightenment." By integrating their knowledge of all Buddha's teachings into their practice of Lamrim, and by integrating this into their everyday lives, Kadampa Buddhists are encouraged to use Buddha's teachings as practical methods for transforming daily activities into the path to enlightenment. The great Kadampa Teachers are famous not only for being great scholars, but also for being spiritual practitioners of immense purity and sincerity.

The lineage of these teachings, both their oral transmission and blessings, was then passed from Teacher to disciple, spreading throughout much of Asia, and now to many countries throughout the Western world. Buddha's teachings, which are known as *Dharma*, are likened to a wheel that moves from country to country in accordance with changing conditions and people's karmic inclinations. The external forms of presenting Buddhism may change as it meets with different cultures and societies, but its essential authenticity is ensured through the continuation of an unbroken lineage of realized practitioners.

Kadampa Buddhism was first introduced into the West in 1977 by the renowned Buddhist Master, Venerable Geshe Kelsang Gyatso. Since that time, he has worked tirelessly to spread Kadampa Buddhism throughout the world by giving extensive teachings, writing many profound texts on Kadampa Buddhism, and founding the New Kadampa Tradition—International Kadampa Buddhist Union (NKT-IKBU), which now has over a thousand Kadampa Buddhist Centers and groups worldwide. Each Center offers study programs on Buddhist psychology, philosophy, and meditation instruction, as well as retreats for all levels of practitioner. The emphasis is on integrating Buddha's teachings into daily life to solve our human problems and to spread lasting peace and happiness throughout the world.

The Kadampa Buddhism of the NKT-IKBU is an entirely independent Buddhist tradition and has no political affiliations. It is an association of Buddhist Centers and practitioners that derive their inspiration and guidance from the example of the ancient Kadampa Buddhist Masters and their teachings, as presented by Geshe Kelsang Gyatso.

There are three reasons why we need to study and practice the teachings of Buddha: to develop our wisdom, to cultivate a good heart, and to maintain a peaceful state of mind. If we do not strive to develop our wisdom, we will always remain ignorant of ultimate truth—the true nature of reality. Although we wish for happiness, our ignorance leads us to engage in non-virtuous actions, which are the main cause of all our suffering. If we do not cultivate a good heart, our selfish motivation destroys harmony and good relationships with others. We have no peace, and no chance to gain pure happiness. Without inner peace, outer peace is impossible. If we do not maintain a peaceful state of mind, we are not happy even if we have ideal conditions. On the other hand, when our mind is peaceful, we are happy, even if our external conditions are unpleasant. Therefore, the development of these qualities is of utmost importance for our daily happiness.

Geshe Kelsang Gyatso, or *Geshe-la* as he is affectionately called by his students, has designed three special spiritual programs for the systematic study and practice of Kadampa Buddhism that are especially suited to the modern world—the General Program (GP), the Foundation Program (FP), and the Teacher Training Program (TTP).

GENERAL PROGRAM

The General Program provides a basic introduction to Buddhist view, meditation, and practice that is suitable for beginners. It also includes advanced teachings and practice from both Sutra and Tantra.

FOUNDATION PROGRAM

The Foundation Program provides an opportunity to deepen our understanding and experience of Buddhism through a systematic study of six texts:

1. *Joyful Path of Good Fortune*—a commentary to Atisha's Lamrim instructions, the stages of the path to enlightenment.
2. *Universal Compassion*—a commentary to Bodhisattva Chekhawa's *Training the Mind in Seven Points.*
3. *Eight Steps to Happiness*—a commentary to Bodhisattva Langri Tangpa's *Eight Verses of Training the Mind.*

4. *Heart of Wisdom*—a commentary to the *Heart Sutra*.

5. *Meaningful to Behold*—a commentary to Venerable Shantideva's *Guide to the Bodhisattva's Way of Life*.

6. *Understanding the Mind*—a detailed explanation of the mind, based on the works of the Buddhist scholars Dharmakirti and Dignaga.

The benefits of studying and practicing these texts are as follows:

(1) *Joyful Path of Good Fortune*—we gain the ability to put all Buddha's teachings of both Sutra and Tantra into practice. We can easily make progress on, and complete, the stages of the path to the supreme happiness of enlightenment. From a practical point of view, Lamrim is the main body of Buddha's teachings, and the other teachings are like its limbs.

(2) and (3) *Universal Compassion* and *Eight Steps to Happiness*— we gain the ability to integrate Buddha's teachings into our daily life and solve all our human problems.

(4) *Heart of Wisdom*—we gain a realization of the ultimate nature of reality. By gaining this realization, we can eliminate the ignorance of self-grasping, which is the root of all our suffering.

(5) *Meaningful to Behold*—we transform our daily activities into the Bodhisattva's way of life, thereby making every moment of our human life meaningful.

(6) *Understanding the Mind*—we understand the relationship between our mind and its external objects. If we understand that objects depend on the subjective mind, we can change the way objects appear to us by changing our own mind. Gradually we will gain the ability to control our mind and in this way solve all our problems.

TEACHER TRAINING PROGRAM

The Teacher Training Program is designed for people who wish to train as authentic Dharma Teachers. In addition to completing the study of fourteen texts of Sutra and Tantra, which include the six texts mentioned above, students are required to observe certain commitments with regard to behavior and way of life, and to complete a number of meditation retreats.

All Kadampa Buddhist Centers are open to the public. Every year we celebrate Festivals in many countries throughout the world, including the USA and England, where people gather from around the world to receive special teachings and empowerments and to enjoy a spiritual vacation. Please feel free to visit us any time!

For further information, please contact:

US NKT–IKBU Office
Kadampa Meditation Center New York
47 Sweeney Road
Glen Spey, NY 12737, USA

Phone: 845-856-9000
Toll free: 877-523-2672
Fax: 845-856-2110
Email: info@KadampaNewYork.org
Website: www.KadampaNewYork.org

or

NKT–IKBU Central Office
Conishead Priory
Ulverston, Cumbria, LA12 9QQ, England

Phone: (0) 1229-588533
Fax: (0) 1229-580080
Email: info@kadampa.org
Website: www.kadampa.org

Tharpa Publications Worldwide

*B*ooks from Tharpa Publications are currently available in American English, British English, Chinese, French, German, Italian, Japanese, Portuguese, and Spanish. Most languages are available from any Tharpa Publications office listed below.

Tharpa Publications USA
47 Sweeney Road
Glen Spey, NY 12737
USA
Phone: 845-856-5102
Toll-free: 888-741-3475
Fax: 845-856-2110
Web: www.tharpa.com/us/
E-mail: info.us@tharpa.com

Tharpa Publications Canada
631 Crawford Street
Toronto, ON M6G 3K1
CANADA
Phone: 905-274-1842
Toll-free: 866-523-2672
Fax: 905-274-1714
Web: www.tharpa.com/ca/
E-mail: info.ca@tharpa.com

Tharpa Publications UK
Conishead Priory
Ulverston
Cumbria, LA12 9QQ
UNITED KINGDOM
Phone: +44 (0)1229-588599
Fax: +44 (0)1229-483919
Web: www.tharpa.com/uk/
E-mail: info.uk@tharpa.com

Tharpa Publications Australia
PO Box 63
Monbulk, Vic 3793
AUSTRALIA
Phone: +61 (3) 9752-0377
Web: www.tharpa.com/au/
E-mail: info.au@tharpa.com

Editorial Tharpa Brasil
Rua Fradique Coutinho 710
Vila Madalena
05416-011 São Paulo - SP
BRAZIL
Phone/Fax: +55 (11) 3812 7509
Web: www.budismo.org.br
E-mail: info.br@tharpa.com

Tharpa Asia
Flat H, 4th Floor, Bo Wah Mansion
54 Queen's Road East
Wanchai
HONG KONG
Phone: +852 25205137
Fax: +852 25072208
Web: www.tharpa.com/hk-cht/
E-mail: info.hk@tharpa.com

Tharpa Verlag
Mirabellenstrasse 1
8048 Zurich
SWITZERLAND
Phone: +41 44 401 02 20
Fax: +41 44 461 36 88
Web: www.tharpa.com/ch/
E-mail: info.ch@tharpa.com

Editions Tharpa
Château de Segrais
72220 Saint-Mars-d'Outillé
FRANCE
Phone: +33 (0)2 43 87 71 02
Fax : +33 (0)2 76 01 34 10
Web: www.tharpa.com/fr/
E-mail: info.fr@tharpa.com

Editorial Tharpa España
Camino Fuente del Perro s/n
29120 Alhaurín el Grande (Málaga)
SPAIN
Phone: +34 952 596808
Fax: +34 952 490175
Web: www.tharpa.com/es/
E-mail: info.es@tharpa.com

Index

death 19–22, 30, 51–55, 58, 94
  meditation 53–55
  sufferings of 74
death, intermediate state, and rebirth 19–21
dedication 96, 167
degenerate times 112
delusion 15–16, 40, 46, 59–60, 65–66, 116–17, 133
  innate 140–41
  intellectually-formed 138
demi-gods 31, 115
demon 8–9
desire realm 115–16
desires, failing to satisfy 76–78
Devaputra Mara 8–9
Dharma 11, 57, 59–60, 148–50, 150–51.
  See also Buddhadharma; Dharma practice; Wheel of Dharma
  meaning of 11
  scriptures 149
Dharmapala 23, 24
Dharma practice 11, 55, 72,

Dharma practice *(continued)* 74, 109, 112–14
  essence of 16, 45
divisive speech 34, 35
dreams 19–21, 22–24, 31, 133
dualistic appearance 137–38, 141

E

effort 110–14.
  See also six perfections
  three types 113
emanations 9, 142–43
emptiness 79–82, 123–33.
  See also ultimate nature; ultimate truth; wisdom realizing emptiness
  direct realization 116, 118, 120
  of the body 130–32
  of the I 124–29
enemy 105
enlightened being.
  See Buddha
enlightenment 85, 135–43, 152
exalted wisdom 140
exalted wisdom of the final continuum 141

N

Further Reading

If you have enjoyed reading this book and would like to find out more about Buddhist thought and practice, here are some other books by Geshe Kelsang Gyatso that you might like to read. They are all available from Tharpa Publications.

HOW TO SOLVE OUR HUMAN PROBLEMS

The Four Noble Truths

When things go wrong in our life and we encounter difficult situations, we tend to regard the situation itself as our problem, but in reality whatever problems we experience come from the side of the mind. If we responded to difficult situations with a positive or peaceful mind they would not be problems for us. Eventually, we might even regard them as challenges or opportunities for growth and development. Problems arise only if we respond to difficulties with a negative state of mind. Therefore if we want to be free from problems, we must transform our mind.

"Geshe Kelsang Gyatso has a unique gift for addressing everyday difficulties."
   —*American Library Association's Booklist*

"This book offers peace of mind in these troubled times."
   —*Publishing News, UK*

TRANSFORM YOUR LIFE

A Blissful Journey

By following the practical advice given in this book, we can transform our mind and our life, fulfill our human potential, and find everlasting peace and happiness.

"A practical guide to transforming one's life by understanding the nature of love."
—Library Journal

THE NEW MEDITATION HANDBOOK

A Practical Guide to Buddhist Meditation

This popular and practical manual allows us to discover for ourselves the inner peace and lightness of mind that come from meditation. The author explains twenty-one step-by-step meditations that lead to increasingly beneficial states of mind, and that together form the entire Buddhist path to enlightenment.

"This manual provides a succinct and inspiring overview of the many ways in which Budhism can be applied to the situations and activities of daily life."
—Spirituality & Health

EIGHT STEPS TO HAPPINESS

The Buddhist Way of Loving Kindness

This inspiring book reveals deeply transforming, yet practical methods to enable a powerful opening of the heart, the source of all true happiness. It explains how to meditate on eight beautiful verses that comprise one of Buddhism's best-loved and most enduring teachings, *Eight Verses of Training the Mind*.

". . . induces calmness and compassion into one's being."
  —*New Humanity Journal.*

JOYFUL PATH OF GOOD FORTUNE

The Complete Buddhist Path to Enlightenment

Step-by-step guidance on all the meditations that lead to limitless peace and happiness. Enriched with stories and analogies, the author presents with great clarity all Buddha's teachings in the order in which they are practiced. Following these instructions, we will come to experience for ourselves the joy that arises from making progress on a clear and structured path to enlightenment.

"This book is invaluable."
  —*World Religions in Education.*

UNIVERSAL COMPASSION

Transforming Your Life through Love and Compassion

In a book whose warmth and immediacy speak directly to our lives, ancient meditative techniques are brought alive for a modern audience and made relevant to our everyday experiences. This immensely readable book will have a remarkable impact on our life.

"An inspiring book."
—*Buddhist Studies Review*

ℰℑ

Our books are available in most bookstores. To request a catalog, or to order books directly from Tharpa Pubications, please contact us (see page 191).